“What if you could find a fruit tree that produced a fruit with nine brilliantly colored flavors? What if the tree grew along the roadside and was available to everybody? Would you be drawn to that tree? Would the tree pull you to it like a magnet?

Harvey Katz is such a tree. When people experience Harvey, they ‘Taste and see that the Lord is good’ (Psalm 34:8). The flavors are all there. You can’t miss the love, the joy, the peace, the patience, the kindness, the goodness, the faithfulness, the gentleness, the self-control. Of all the people I know, Harvey stands out as ‘a tree planted by the rivers of water, that brings forth his fruit in his season’ (Psalm 1:3). Harvey is well qualified to write this book.”

—David Mainse, Founder of Crossroads Christian Communications and host of *100 Huntley Street*

Becoming a
God
Magnet

Becoming a God Magnet

Life Lessons In Sharing Your Faith

Harvey Katz

Believe Books
Life Stories That Inspire
Washington, DC

BECOMING A GOD MAGNET
By Harvey Katz

Any portions of Scripture which are printed in bold font have been highlighted by the author for emphasis.

ISBN: 0–9787428–9–3

Library of Congress Control Number: 2006933290

Cover design: *Jack Kotowicz, Washington, DC, VelocityDesignGroup.com*
Layout design: *Jen Anderson*

Believe Books publishes the inspirational life stories of extraordinary believers in God from around the world. Requests for information should be addressed to **Believe Books** at **www.believebooks.com**. **Believe Books** is a registered trade name of **Believe Books, LLC** of Washington, D.C.

Printed in the United States of America

To my precious wife, Diane, who has been such a wonderful friend, mother and partner in ministry. Her gift of hospitality and loving kindness has made our home a spiritual haven and a place where many have found Jesus.

And to our wonderful children: Jessica, Michelle and Joshua, who have embraced our love of God and our ministry of reaching out to others with the message of the Gospel.

CONTENTS

FOREWORD

I first met Harvey Katz on Friday, October 10, 1986. I remember because it changed my life and my witness for the Lord forever!

Harvey's life brings a fresh wind of the Spirit from heaven. He has such a way of saying things about the Lord that when he begins to talk, you want to listen. When he begins to teach, it flows. If you want to know about what it means to have liberty in communicating thoughts about God and His Kingdom then meet Harvey. He's one of a kind and gifted to share out of his life. It is not theory, not dry material, but life-giving help, principles and directives.

If you want your mind washed of the old and born into the new, then hear his heart in this book. You will not be neutral by the time you finish reading—you'll either jump in or out—but you won't be the same! Need I say that there is more than Harvey at work here. There is the gentle touch of the "Hound of Heaven" who desires all men, women, boys and girls to come to the knowledge of salvation.

We are all called to be witnesses, but Harvey is called to be a witness to the witnesses, a teacher to the teachers, and a mentor to the mentors.

I cherish our friendship, I honor his calling and I recommend this tiny portion of his life's testimony to you.

In love and gratitude forever,

Clyde Williamson
Director of Operation Outreach and the Israel PrayerWatch

ACKNOWLEDGMENTS

I would like to thank Elizabeth Stalcup for her perseverance and her encouragement in helping me to refine the material in this book, Shirley Howson for her thorough and careful editing and George and Gretchen Keitt for their final pre-publication readiing of the text.

A GOD MAGNET?
WHAT IS A GOD MAGNET?

It all started when my kids were young. We were riding in the car. My daughter and one of her friends were talking in the back seat. "He's a chick magnet," one of them said. They were talking about a boy in their class, who was apparently creating quite a stir among the fourth graders.

> *A chick magnet*, I thought. *I want to be a God magnet! I want to draw people to Jesus.*

That is what this book is all about . . .

EVERYONE (EVEN YOU) CAN DRAW PEOPLE TO JESUS

> And I, if and when I am lifted up from the earth [on the cross], will draw and attract all men [Gentiles as well as Jews] to Myself.
>
> —John 12:32 AMP

Many Christians view evangelism as a chore, a responsibility they dread. They think they have to argue with people to get them "saved." This puts them under undue pressure, and makes them feel defeated when they don't see results. Many Christians simply say, "I'm not called to be an evangelist." They don't want to be bothered, preferring to leave evangelism to the pastor or someone else.

The truth is, God wants to use *all* of His children—even you—to reach other people with the Good News of Jesus Christ! I hope this will encourage you. God has not given this privilege to angels but to His Church. Those who are truly His children have the wonderful opportunity to pass the Good News on to others. Indeed we all have a responsibility to do so. What a joy it is to pray with someone to receive Jesus as their Savior and Lord!

You may not be as gifted an evangelist as someone else you know, but God wants to attract non-believers to Jesus Christ *through your life*. You are meant to be a "God magnet." That is what this book is about: Letting Jesus live His life through you so that you bring others to Christ.

As we lift up Jesus, He will attract people to Himself. He does the work through you and through me. Every Christian can draw people to Jesus, because of who He is in us. Everyone needs Jesus and everyone deserves an opportunity to hear about Him.

I remember the peace I experienced when I first came to Christ. It was truly "joy unspeakable and full of glory" (1 Peter 1:8, KJV). In my early years as a Christian, I experienced such joy when God answered my simple prayers or when I read Scripture and found precious insights in His Word. I felt blessed to know God. It was this early experience of God's joy that motivated me to tell others the Good News about Jesus Christ—His life, death and resurrection and the eternal life He offers to those who receive Him.

I was lost and in darkness before Jesus became my Savior and Lord. It was wonderful to discover that Jesus offered me the amazing gift of eternal life. I just had to share it with others. I was "bursting at the seams!" A friend and I began witnessing for Christ in our high school. Much to my amazement, people starting giving their lives to Jesus Christ. It is true that some rejected our message (and us), but that was a small price to pay for the wonderful results we witnessed among those who believed!

That was over 30 years ago. Since then, I have had the privilege of sharing my faith with many others. I marvel at how the Spirit of God touches and transforms lives. I have seen and experienced both the joys and disappointments of sharing my faith, and through these experiences I want to share with you what I learned along the way.

When it comes to evangelism, we don't have to ask God if He wants us to share our faith. He has already made that clear in His Word. My friend Pastor Jay puts it this way, "Two thirds of God's name is 'Go.'" The Great Commission is based on Matthew 28:18–20:

> "All authority has been given to Me in heaven and on earth. **Go therefore and make disciples of all the nations,** baptizing them in the name of the Father and of the Son and of the Holy Spirit, teaching them to observe all things that I have commanded you; and lo, I am with you always, *even* to the end of the age." Amen.

This book is not so much a "how to" book, as an opportunity to look at the Word of God and see principles to be learned about sharing our faith. I use personal examples to illustrate my experiences. This does not mean that we don't use methods for sharing our faith; to the contrary, there are some excellent tools that I will discuss toward the end of the book. What I want to do is teach you how you can share your faith with others effectively, so that you know when and how to use the available tools.

The book has three themes:

1. Identification—Speaking to the Heart
2. Preparation—You are a Life Message
3. Presentation—One Message, Many Methods.

We have tremendous freedom in Christ. God has called us to freedom! I have known many believers who are scared to death to evangelize or who find it a great burden. You may be one of them! You know you should share your faith, but you never feel especially capable or comfortable doing so. I want to encourage you, and pray that this book will be a blessing to you.

CHAPTER 1

HOW A NICE JEWISH BOY BECAME A FOLLOWER OF JESUS

No self-respecting Jew would willingly become a "Christian." So how did a nice Jewish boy like me come to believe that Jesus is the Messiah? Let me share my story.

I was born at the end of the baby boom generation, in 1959, during that quiet lull after WWII and before the Beatles, Vietnam and the "free love era" of sex, drugs and "rock n' roll." My father, who was 42 years old when I was born, was a survivor of the Mauthausen concentration camp in Austria. His young adult years had been spent in hellish work camps and in the dreaded Mauthausen, just trying with all his might to survive. He endured such terrible hardships at the hands of the Nazis that he was literally skin and bones when he was liberated in May 1945 at the age of 28. What was the crime for which he was he imprisoned? Nothing other than the fact that my father was Jewish.

His survival was miraculous. Many times, unexplainable events kept him alive when he was near the point of death. On one occasion a rainstorm drenched the prisoners while they were being moved from one camp to another. They shivered in the cold, but in the morning, to everyone's astonishment, the ground was covered with snails. They were so many that they could not see the underlying grass, only a sea of brownish gray snails—in such abundance that several thousand malnourished prisoners filled their bellies by boiling and eating them. My father said it was like manna from heaven. When I think about this and other times that God provided for my father in the camps, my only explanation is that God had a purpose for his life.

After the war my father returned to his native Slovakia, but soon the Communists seized power. He had to get out of Eastern Europe; his life there was over, so along with thousands of other Jews, he immigrated to Canada to start a new life, with new hopes and dreams. In 1949, at the age of 32, he arrived at Halifax Harbor with very little money, no immediate family, and almost no knowledge of English.

Eventually he settled in London, Ontario where he met my mother. They married on July 11, 1954. My mother was an only child, born and reared in Canada, the daughter of Jewish parents who left Poland before the Holocaust. My father's family were strict Orthodox Jews, while my mother's parents were more liberal in their Judaism, mainly attending services on the High Holidays.

My older brother, Howard, was born in October of 1955. I came along four years later, and then, five years after I arrived, our family was blessed with a baby sister, Priscilla. Howard and I were both circumcised as infants by a *mohel*—a Rabbi who performs the ceremonial rites of circumcision. Each of us was named after a relative who had died before our birth.

Names are extremely important in the Jewish culture. It is customary to name children after deceased relatives to keep their memory alive. This became especially important for those whose relatives perished in the Holocaust.

I was named after my paternal grandfather *Herschel* and my maternal grandfather *Moishe*. My English name *Harvey Martin* is what is recorded on my birth certificate but my Yiddish name is *Moishe Herschele*. Many Jewish people have two sets of names, an English set and a Hebrew or Yiddish set.

I grew up in a city with a small, yet influential, Jewish community. When I was six years old a strange man wearing dark clothes and a long black beard came to our home to speak with my father. He explained that he was starting a Jewish day school in our city and he needed five children to start the school. He asked my father to let me to be one of those five students.

My father agreed and that fall I started second grade at the London Hebrew Day School. We studied the Hebrew language and Jewish studies in the morning and regular subjects in the afternoon. I learned to read Hebrew and this became the basis for our daily prayers that we recited from our *Siddur*, or prayer book, each morning at the start of class.

We studied our great culture and heritage with pride. We developed a sense of our lineage, which extended all the way back to our Patriarch Abraham, the first Jew. I remember feeling privileged to be part of a great story of redemption. Our family name is *Katz*, which comes from two Hebrew words meaning "Righteous Priest." According to tradition we are the descendants of Aaron the High Priest, Moses' brother.

Jewish identity is bound up in being part of the community. As Jews, each one of us carries a collective responsibility for our culture and community. Prayer is offered to God by a group of at least ten men called a

Minyan. We pray by reciting prayers from the *Siddur*, in concert with the nine other men who make up the Minyan.

For Jewish communities to function properly the group must have a synagogue for prayer along with the minimum ten men mentioned earlier. We also need kosher meat; a ritual bath called a *Mikvah* where those who are ceremonially unclean can wash themselves; and a Rabbi and a Cantor. The Rabbi, or "teacher," is the spiritual leader of the Jewish community. His primary role is to teach the Jewish laws and customs to his people.

The Cantor is a person who leads the congregation in singing. A substantial amount of training is required to be able to recite the prescribed prayers, Psalms, and readings from the Torah. The musical notations are quite different from our Western sounds and rhythms.

In front of the Holy Ark is the *Bema* where the Cantor leads the congregation in prayers and where the Torah Scrolls are brought out during the reading of the Law. It is quite a ceremony to bring out the scrolls and parade them around the synagogue before they are opened and read in front of the congregation. Afterward the scrolls are rolled back up and placed into the Ark and the door or curtain is closed. The whole service revolves around this ritual and the service ends shortly after the Torah is returned to its place.

The Rabbi addresses the congregation with a short sermon called a *Drasha*. He will comment on the reading of the Torah portion for that morning and will try to find an application for the congregation to think about. Sometimes he will try to relate it to current events. Other times, the sermon will speak of Jewish responsibility in a secular world. I would always leave the synagogue with a renewed sense of responsibility to keep my Jewish heritage alive.

According to Jewish custom, a young man or young woman is held accountable for his or her own actions at the age of puberty. This occasion is marked by a Bar Mitzvah for boys and a Bat Mitzvah for girls. Before I had my Bar Mitzvah, I spent a couple of years preparing to recite my Torah and *Haftorah* portion in the synagogue. These are the weekly readings out of the Bible, and it is customary for a young man when he comes of age to recite these readings in public. It was the Cantor who spent time with me, teaching me how to sing my allotted portion.

The Bar Mitzvah is an occasion that brings both privilege and responsibility. Coming of age is serious, but reaching that milestone is also cause for joy and celebration. After the ceremony in the synagogue, the young man (or woman in the case of a Bat Mitzvah) is honored with a celebration—singing, dancing, and delicious food followed by speeches from family members and distinguished guests.

A couple of hundred people attended my Bar Mitzvah. A Jewish band from Toronto played for the celebration. I was showered with gifts and money. My father and mother were so proud of me. The occasion was quite an honor.

The reason I mention all of this is so you can understand that being Jewish is much more than a belief system; it is an identity. The population of the world is currently about six billion, and of those, world Jewry numbers only about fifteen million, a fraction of one percent. The Jewish people have survived countless persecutions and onslaughts. Thousands were forced to convert to Christianity, or were killed during the Inquisition. Organized *mob raids* in the nineteenth and twentieth centuries in Poland and Russia called "pogroms" devastated Jewish communities, and the unthinkable Holocaust murdered six million Jews.

It was into this sense of Jewish identity that I was born and brought up. Christianity to me was always forbidden territory, which I neither wanted nor would be permitted to enter. My father always respected Christians, or any other religion for that matter, but *we were Jews!* I had a strong sense of responsibility to carry on the Jewish tradition. Becoming a Christian did not even cross my mind; it would have been unthinkable!

No self-respecting Jew would apostatize willingly and become a "Christian." One of the words used for such a person is *geshmat*, which means "to destroy." Such a person would be called a *meshumad*, which means "one who has abandoned his faith." When it came to conversion, we Jews used strong language to express strong feelings. To become a *meshumad* meant betraying your people and your history. Four thousand years of Jewish culture and religion—finished! Conversion would defile your heritage just as Esau despised his birthright.

This was my understanding and experience of Judaism. Ours was a heritage to protect, a responsibility to ensure the future survival of our people. How could I think of betraying my people after all the Jewish people had suffered? What about the names of my ancestors? What about the shame and embarrassment to my parents and the whole Jewish community? How could I even *consider* the unthinkable?

My faith journey did not begin with a desire or interest to become a follower of Jesus. After my Bar Mitzvah I wanted to know the true, living God of Israel. I was not looking for Jesus! Jesus was the Savior of the Gentiles, not the Jews. I was looking for *God*. I had been too well educated to buy into "Jesus stuff" and besides my Jewish identity and conscience would never allow me to stray over to the "other side." Or so I thought.

One of the things I had learned about God from my Jewish heritage is that God is *Kadosh*, which means "holy." God is so holy that His name, as it is written in the Bible and prayer books, is never spoken. Some translations of God's name into English are "Jehovah" or "Yahweh." I had never heard of these names growing up. In prayer the name of God is read *Adonai* which means "Lord" and this is even noted in many translations of the Bible in all capital letters: LORD. When God is spoken of conversationally, He is referred to as *HaShem*, which means "The Name." It was this sense of God's holiness that kept me distant from Him—from knowing God personally. While I was growing up I had never heard of having a personal relationship with God. Such a concept had not entered my mind. I didn't know such a thing was possible.

I had learned to have great respect for God and His holiness as a young Jewish man. When I went to the synagogue to say prayers, I felt I was doing serious business with God. I prayed liturgically through prescribed prayers in our *Siddur*. I read these prayers phonetically because I didn't understand enough Hebrew to translate them for myself. Hebrew was *loshen kodesh*, which means a "holy language."

Prayer was not something that I understood but rather a duty to be performed. I wasn't expecting to get something out of prayer; it was something I was required to offer up to God. When we prayed we always faced toward the front of the synagogue, which faced east toward Jerusalem.

But something happened to me after my Bar Mitzvah. I can't say exactly what it was or when it started, but I began to search for God. At night I would go to bed and wonder, *Where is God? What is He like?* I was filled with questions. *Was there really a God or not?* Schools were teaching evolution so I wondered, *Where did God fit into that? If there is a God, why did He allow the Holocaust? Is there life after death?*

These thoughts continued for many months after my Bar Mitzvah. I believed I was now responsible for my own sins. Would I be good enough to have *Chayim B'Olam Habah*—"Eternal life?" You had to be "good enough" to get to heaven when you died. God kept a record of your deeds, and if your good deeds exceeded your bad deeds you went to heaven when you died, but if your bad deeds exceeded your good deeds then you went to hell. This was risky business!

Eventually I came to the conclusion that of course there must be a God, but He was an angry God. *Wouldn't you be angry with all those people running around sinning when you told them not to?* I thought that life's tragedies were the result of something having gone wrong in the universe. That something was sin, so everything wrong with the world was the direct or indirect result of sin. For instance, stealing would be a sin against another person because that person would not deserve it. Sin hurts people. Similarly sacrilege would be a sin against God—and that is *serious* business.

I thought that I needed to work on my negative balance by performing more *good deeds* ("mitzvahs") so that I could earn my right to enter heaven by the time I died. As I became more aware of God's holiness, I also became more aware of my own sinful heart. I knew that I had lied and done wrong things in the past, but now it seemed that every sin was becoming more obvious. Pride, disrespect, lying, and many other sins were rearing their ugly heads. The more I tried to overcome them, the more I was overcome!

One time when I was in the synagogue praying, I was overcome with a sense of being so empty. I mouthed the words to the prayers. They were beautiful, yet they seemed so foreign and God seemed unreachable. With great sadness I put down the prayer book, and in my heart I said to God, "Oh God, where are You?" Without realizing it, I had prayed one of my first heartfelt prayers to God. Nothing happened. I went home feeling that I would never be certain of my salvation or even know if God could be reached.

I came to the conclusion that God was too holy for me, but I hoped that one day—with a lot of work—I might be holy enough to please God. I was in despair because there was no way to know for sure. I became convinced of one thing: if there were a God, then my sin was separating me from Him, but I had no clue how to overcome my sin.

I cannot remember how long I stayed in this depressed state, perhaps a couple of years. It was not something I talked about with anyone. My inner world was in turmoil, while my outer world of friends and school appeared normal. I was never a "good" student, but I got by. Most of my friends in high school were not Jewish, so I didn't speak much about religion. And our home was a place where we never spoke about God. We spoke about being Jewish—but not about God.

I was afraid to talk about God. It was too personal—even with my own family—and I knew deep down they didn't have the answers either. My sense of despair would wax and wane, but never disappear. I tried to find satisfaction in fishing or nature, or fun with my friends, but the emptiness and loneliness was always there lurking beneath the surface. When I was alone with my thoughts, I wrestled with the big issues of life and death, tormented by my lack of answers about the meaning and purpose of life.

I was trapped in a prison and didn't know how to get out, or who held the key. My prison was invisible to anyone on the outside, but very real to me, the prisoner within. It was a prison of loneliness and fear, but the feeling of emptiness was the worst part. I longed to go to sleep at night to escape my misery.

May 3, 1976 changed my life forever. My brother Howard had a new white Fiat and would be leaving home the next day to take a job in sewer construction for several months. We hopped in the car to take a ride.

I was sitting in the back seat with Howard's friend, Hank. Howard had another buddy beside him in the front. I remember Howard saying to Hank, "Please don't talk about religion." That caught my attention. As we were driving around in his car that night, in the country, I looked at the clouds and sky and marveled at their beauty. I nonchalantly remarked, "I wonder if there is a God?" I don't recall if I was even expecting an answer; it was more a statement of wonder and awe.

Hank was quick to comment, "There *is* and I know Him." I was astonished! How could one possibly *know* God? What does it mean to know God? What an introduction! That evening we ended up at my home in my basement, just Hank and me. I was excited because I had been hoping all evening for a chance to question Hank alone.

Hank was very gracious and non-judgmental. I remember telling him my "theory" about God and how we need to be good enough to get to heaven when we die. He simply and gently said, "You will never be good enough." That simple statement resonated deep within my soul. I knew he was absolutely correct, because I had failed to achieve perfection. I knew deep down inside that I had failed God, and that God was too holy for me to stand in His presence.

"How can I be made right with God?" I blurted, from the depths of my agonized heart. I was perplexed. *If good deeds aren't good enough what is?* It was the question of all questions. It was the moment I had been longing for—the moment for which I had been destined. I anxiously waited to hear and understand what his answer would be. *Would it mean my eternal doom? Was there any hope at all?* I must have felt like a person waiting for the doctor's prognosis regarding a serious illness. *Is this terminal*? But this was far more important than even a human diagnosis of an illness because I was waiting for an answer regarding my eternal destiny.

I remember sensing that God was present in the room in a way that I had never felt before. It is difficult to describe, and I have not felt the same intensity since that evening. I was standing at the door of eternity and for a moment, time stood still. *Would I be accepted or rejected? What did God think of me? Was He angry with me because of my failures and sins?*

Hank shared the truth with me boldly. I was all ears. "You never will be good enough, but God sent His Son Jesus Christ, the Messiah, to be a sacrifice for your sins—so that if you repent of your sins and accept Jesus Christ as your Savior, you will be saved." I remember thinking two things: the first was that this was the truth because it was the only explanation that made sense to me, and the second was that if I rejected this offer I might never have another opportunity. I quickly agreed to pray to receive Jesus as my Savior and Lord. No matter what, I could not turn back now that I had found what I had been waiting for. Yes, I wanted to accept Jesus as my Savior.

Hank told me that he would pray a prayer on my behalf and if I said "Amen" in agreement with his prayer it would be the same as if I had prayed the prayer myself. This is one of the ways we prayed in the synagogue; the Cantor would pray a prayer and the congregation would say, "Amen." He prayed a prayer acknowledging my sin and inability to save myself, receiving Jesus as my sacrifice and Savior, thanking God for sending Jesus to die for my sins and raising Him from the dead. When he finished praying I lifted my head and wanted to express what was in my heart, but not knowing how, I exclaimed, "I believe, I believe!"

We went out for a walk that night, and as we walked I felt an incredible supernatural peace wash over me in waves. It was like being saturated in liquid love. At the time, I felt only euphoria. The long journey ahead with many trials, temptations, and pitfalls was still to come, but that night I simply enjoyed a peace that I had not experienced before. Later, I wondered, *What about my family? What about my Jewish community? What will they think?*

In a funny sort of way I felt more Jewish than ever. I had grown up hearing the great stories of my ancestors and their relationship with God. Now I felt a deeper connection to the God of Abraham, Isaac and Jacob. I felt that I had become a true son of Abraham.

Howard left the next morning to work up north and I didn't see him again until the end of the summer. A few nights after he left, I got down on my hands and knees in front of my home and committed my family to God. It was more an act of desperation than faith, but God has honored it. Howard came to faith in Christ that summer, and eventually my whole family trusted in Jesus.

One of the things that has stayed with me over the years is the deep appreciation for my salvation experience, and my desire to share Christ with others. This book is born out of a lifetime of experiences and sharing. It has been forged out of the fires and trials of life, as well as the glory of victories. Through it all, God has been faithful and He alone deserves the glory. May you be encouraged as you read these pages, and may you allow God to use you to become a "God magnet."

CHAPTER 2

THE RESULTS ARE UP TO GOD

This book is about principles of evangelism. The word *principle* refers to the basic way that something works. Principles also imply a process—which is not always completed in an instant. Coming to faith in God often takes time. When a person responds quickly to the Gospel, God has often been at work for some time. There are exceptions, but the process is usually slow.

God uses many things to speak to the heart of a person about their need for the Savior. He uses circumstances. He works invisibly behind the scenes by His Spirit. He works visibly through His Word, the Bible, and He works through interactions with believers.

Paul put it this way, "I planted the seed, Apollos watered it, but God made it grow. So neither he who plants nor he who waters is anything, but only God, who makes things grow" (1 Corinthians 3:6–7, NIV). Notice how Paul uses the illustration of gardening. In a garden someone puts the seed or plant in the ground. Someone else may water and someone else may harvest the garden. It may be one person who does all these things or it may involve several people.

Did you notice that Paul said, "God gives the increase?" It is important to understand that salvation is the work of God. We co-labor together with Christ in His work, but the results are God's alone. We can take no credit for the salvation of other people. Christ alone paid the price for our salvation on the cross, and He regenerates us by His Spirit. In that sense, we never "save" people.

At the same time, we have a part to play in the process of leading people to faith in Jesus Christ. We present the truth, so they can respond to the Spirit's invitation. The key is to understand that we have a part to play in the process of leading people to faith in Jesus Christ. Did you notice that some sow, some water and some harvest? This means that God may use you at any point in the process, but it is His work! Your work, your part in the harvest will be unique to your gifts and calling.

Coming to Christ doesn't happen overnight. Today a tremendous number of people are finding salvation in Africa and China, but this great harvest was preceded by many prayers sown a century earlier by missionary pioneers. Today others are reaping the rewards of their labor. The reason I mention this is because "success" should not be defined by results, but rather by *faithfulness*.

Results are God's business. Faithfulness is our business. In that sense, faithfulness can yield true success. Years after we sow spiritual seed into people's lives, others may bring them to Christ. We must avoid the temptation to feel jealous that we did all the work and now others have the privilege of bringing those individuals to Christ. We should rejoice that we have done our part; now they are doing their part that *together* we may bring in the harvest.

That is what we mean by *process*. Ministering to people requires time and patience. We need to give people time to think and make sure that the decisions they make are truly their own. It may take years to build relationships in order to share the Gospel. There are exceptions to this, of course. For example, a person on his deathbed doesn't have a lot of time; in fact, many people are on the doorstep of eternity and may be taken at any moment, without notice.

Many years ago my brother Howard picked up a hitchhiker, a teenager who was having a "good time" with his life—drinking and "living it up." Howard felt that he was to share his faith in Christ with this teenager. However, Howard dropped him off without sharing. After he let him out of the car, Howard felt that he had missed an opportunity, so he prayed and asked God for a second chance.

When Howard returned from his business appointment a couple of hours later, he met the same hitchhiker looking for a ride back! This time Howard didn't hesitate. He shared with him the precious truths of the Gospel of Jesus Christ. The young man listened intently, and agreed with Howard about his need for Jesus, but felt that accepting Jesus would require a change in lifestyle and he wasn't ready for that! He told Howard that when he was older and nearing the end of his life, he would turn his life over to Christ. Until then, he wanted to "enjoy" life. Two weeks later this young man died tragically in an automobile accident.

Clearly, that young man had no idea that he would soon face his Maker, and only God knows if he received Christ before he died, but what a divine opportunity God provided for him!

The need for the Gospel is urgent, but the method of sharing the Gospel requires patience. People should never feel forced or pushed to accept Christ. We may feel that they need to be pushed, but this is not God's way. We are not to control or manipulate the decisions of others—especially when it comes to matters of faith. Each person must decide for himself.

A friend of mine has this saying: "A person convinced against his will, is of the same opinion still." In other words, some people may pray to receive Christ but if they have done so under compulsion and have not had a change of heart, then nothing of substance happens. It is not the *prayer* that produces the change; it is true repentance and faith in Christ alone that counts.

So relax. You don't have to push or prod. The results are not up to you. If you let the light of Jesus shine in your life, people will be drawn to Jesus. Naturally. Easily. Let me show you how.

PART 1

IDENTIFICATION: *Speaking to the Heart*

> "Comfort, yes, comfort My people!"
> Says your God.
> "Speak comfort to Jerusalem, and cry out to her,
> That her warfare is ended,
> That her iniquity is pardoned;
> For she has received from the LORD's hand
> Double for all her sins."
> —Isaiah 40:1–2

We cannot reach others for God unless we can truly speak to them by identifying or empathizing with who they are and with what might be the cry of their hearts.

In my early years as a Christian, I often argued with people to get them to accept Jesus. My motives were good, but my methods were terrible! Over the years I have never seen an argument produce good fruit. Arguing is often a symptom of pride, an ugly character trait that does not bring glory to God.

This is not to say that there is no place for open and honest discussion of opposing views. We should be willing to engage in discussion with a spirit of humility and love. The problem with arguing is that it fails to deal with the real issues of the heart. We are aiming our sights eighteen inches too high, so to speak—at the head, not the heart. People have reasons for their beliefs, but their motivation needs to be heartfelt and not academic. We don't discard reason, but we recognize that reason must be subject to faith.

CHAPTER 3

WORSHIPING IDOLS

We tend to think of idols as carved pieces of wood or stone that superstitious people used to worship. From the perspective of our "enlightened" generation, Old Testament idol worship seems backward and ignorant. Who would worship a piece of stone or wood today?

But idolatry is much more than bowing before a statue; it is a matter of devotion. Paul addresses idolatry when he says, "put to death your members which are on the earth: fornication, uncleanness, passion, evil desire, and covetousness, which is idolatry" (Colossians 3:5).

"What is covetousness?" The word simply means greed. A greedy person is one who loves money and wants more and more. But covetousness corrupts the whole personality, and can lead to immoral behavior such as stealing, lying, cheating, and even murder.

God is to be the supreme ruler of the human heart; he designed us that way. When someone or something replaces God as the supreme center it is *idolatry*.

Do you see how the heart attitude of a person is reflected in their behavior? The heart is at the root of a person's character; it is what motivates him. If a person loves money, that is what he will worship.

Do you think our modern society has a problem with greed? I think it is one of our biggest pitfalls. Greed is just one example of deep life needs being met by someone or something other than God. The need for money and the necessities of life is legitimate; it is the method of filling that need that makes it idolatry.

We all have needs. God designed us to have needs so we will depend on Him. Our relationship with God is based on our need for Him and His great delight in filling that need in our heart. God doesn't want to withhold His blessing from us; He wants all our needs to be provided through Him. The result of trusting God to supply all our needs is called *contentment*.

Are greedy people content? Do they have peace, joy and happiness? They may have a temporary satisfaction or temporary pleasure from their wealth, but they will never be satisfied with mere things. God didn't leave that option open to us. He designed us to find true peace and contentment in Him and Him alone.

Paul puts it like this,

> Actually, I don't have a sense of needing anything personally. I've learned by now to be quite content whatever my circumstances. I'm just as happy with little as with much, with much as with little. I've found the recipe for being happy whether full or hungry, hands full or hands empty. Whatever I have, wherever I am, I can make it through anything in the One who makes me who I am.
>
> —Philippians 4:11–13, The Message

Jeremiah cries out against the sin of idolatry and its consequences:

> "Has a nation changed *its* gods,
> Which *are* not gods?
> But My people have changed their Glory
> For *what* does not profit.
> Be astonished, O heavens, at this,
> And be horribly afraid;
> Be very desolate," says the LORD.
> "For My people have committed two evils:
> They have forsaken Me, the fountain of living waters,
> *And* hewn themselves cisterns—broken cisterns that
> can hold no water."
> —Jeremiah 2:11–13

Jeremiah denounced the people of Israel for changing gods, for turning from the true living God to things that are not of God. And the consequences for doing so? Jeremiah says that turning to other gods will not profit; it will do harm and not good. It will also produce fear. "Be astonished," he warns, "be horribly afraid."

When Adam and Eve sinned against God in the Garden of Eden, they became afraid. Fear is the result of insecurity in a world without God. When we trust in ourselves and our resources, we find that these quickly come to an end. Some people have more reserves than others—financial, physical, or emotional—but at some point we are all going to face a need we cannot fill.

Jeremiah says that trusting in idols is evil in two ways: we forsake the only true source of living water—God, and we trust in broken cisterns that cannot hold water. Did you notice that we cannot forsake God without trusting in something else? It is impossible. When we forsake God, we *will* trust in idols. The result is always bad—idols cannot hold water; they cannot slake our thirst, neither can they sustain us.

An interesting metaphor is used here. In the desert-like climate of Israel, water is a symbol of life. God is saying to His people, "I am the source of real life." Jesus used this same illustration in John 4:14, when He told the woman at the well that He came to give living water. Idols cannot hold the water that is placed in them.

If we place our trust in something other than God, we will ultimately be disappointed. These disappointments are called *consequences*, and they are the inevitable result of following those things that bring bondage into our lives. Paul refers to those whose "god is their belly," in Philippians 3:19, which says, "whose end is destruction, whose god is their belly, and whose glory is in their shame—who set their mind on earthly things."

Paul is talking about people who are driven by their stomach—the result is destruction and shame. That's strong language. Many people whose "god is their belly" have poor eating habits or eating disorders as a consequence. Billions of health care dollars are spent every year treating preventable conditions related to over or under eating. But we can be free of these cravings. We can experience the spiritual benefits of fasting by setting aside those foods that we crave and focusing instead on God in prayer.

Food is not the only idol in our society. Alcohol, illegal and legal drugs, gambling and other addictive behaviors can be idols. These are just a few examples of the many problems that result from substituting something else for the one true God. The consequence of these behaviors and addictions is always destructive. Food and drink in reasonable proportions, and in appropriate contexts, are good gifts from God.

The needs are legitimate; the question is how to fill them? If we trust in God to provide these things, we can maintain a healthy balance in life.

Whatever we put in the place of the one true God, whatever else we worship, will result in harm. God brought the ten plagues on Egypt, as His judgments on the gods that they worshiped.

> 'For I will pass through the land of Egypt on that night, and will strike all the firstborn in the land of Egypt, both man and beast; and against all the gods of Egypt I will execute judgment: I *am* the LORD.'
>
> —Exodus 12:12

How does God judge us? He gives us what we want! Want to overeat? Overspend? Go ahead, but don't blame God for what happens. When we indulge in something harmful, aren't we the ones to blame? It was our choice—not God's. We only got what we had coming. God wants to deliver us, but we must be willing to let Him do so.

Everyone worships something or someone. Everyone. We need to keep this in mind when we are trying to identify the heartfelt needs of other people. Idolatry will ultimately lead to misery, *but in their misery, we can minister!*—not out of judgment but out of love.

Our own broken places, the areas where we have suffered, can open doors for us to minister to others. We can identify with their plight, because we have been there, too. Knowing our own frailty helps us to see unbelievers with compassion.

CHAPTER 4

BUILDING RELATIONSHIPS

A Relationship of Trust

Before we can minister to others we must build a relationship of trust. We must be trustworthy. This means earning the right to be heard. Love compels us, for love is the foundation for building relationships and sharing our faith with others.

In the New Testament one word for *love* is "agape," which means God's unconditional love for people. It is not based on our ability or behavior. It is based on the character of God. We need to express the heart of God towards others so our love is genuine and sincere.

Love must have no strings attached. Do we love those around us for who they are or do we have an agenda? Are we willing to love others in spite of what they believe, or do we love them only if they agree with us? Early in his ministry, Martin Luther had a love for the Jews—but once they refused to become Christians his love turned to hatred, and this hatred was responsible, in part, for the expulsion of the Jews from Germany. This is a sad example of conditional love and its consequences. We want to love unconditionally.

Are we genuinely interested in the welfare of each person? Do we see them as a project, or do we really want God's best for them? Can we accept them for who they are in spite of their faults and needs? Can we keep a confidence? Can we accept them, not because of what they believe, but because of who they are?

This does not mean we must condone bad behavior. It means wanting to see others set free—regardless of their behavior. Paul tells us to love others without hypocrisy (Romans 12:9). We need to be sincere and genuine in caring for others, even when it requires a sacrifice of time and resources to demonstrate genuine love. One of the best gifts we can give another person is to respectfully listen to them.

Listening with the Heart

Listening is more than being quiet and letting others talk, although that is a good place to start. I believe we need to listen to others *prayerfully*. We need to talk to God while they are talking to us. Only the Holy Spirit can reveal their true needs in His perfect timing. Sometimes it is better to keep our thoughts to ourselves until it is the right moment to share. The person may not be prepared to deal with issues honestly. If we force the discussion, it can damage the relationship, bringing harm instead of good will. Most people do not want you to fix them or solve their problems. They want to be heard and understood.

Listen as you ask God to show you the individual's heart. Lean forward and make eye contact, so they know that you care. Pay attention: What are they feeling and thinking? If that individual knows you are listening, they will begin to open up. Refrain from making snap judgments. Remember, you don't have to have all the answers. No one does except God. Listen and let the other person speak. Trust that God is working in their life, too.

It has been said, "People don't care what you know, until they know how much you care." Paul said in 1 Corinthians 8:1b, "We know that we all have knowledge. Knowledge puffs up, but love edifies." It is love that opens the hearts of others to the knowledge of Christ. When people feel unconditional loved they will trust us.

One person commented that she felt safe with my wife and me; she sensed that we wouldn't judge her for her failures. God wants us to express His love to others so that they can know Him.

In I John 4:18–19 we read, "There is no fear in love; but perfect love casts out fear, because fear involves torment. But he who fears has not been made perfect in love. We love Him because He first loved us." If people are afraid of us, and our message, they will not be able to hear what we are saying about Jesus. We need to demonstrate God's unconditional love for them, before they will be able to trust us—and God.

We have authority in this matter because Scripture says that perfect love casts out fear. People have a lot of fears. My wife and I prayed recently with someone who told us that she was deathly afraid. We assured her, and she trusted us. We prayed with her to receive the Lord, and she had great joy (and so did we!).

We need to love others unconditionally but we also need wisdom. Solomon is a great example of one who asked for wisdom from God. In I Kings 3:9 we read, "Therefore give to Your servant an understanding heart to judge Your people, that I may discern between good and evil. For who is able to judge this great people of Yours?"

The expression *understanding heart* in Hebrew literally means "a hearing heart." Wisdom results in a hearing heart: one that listens attentively with tender compassion. James encourages us to pray for wisdom. "If any of you lacks wisdom, let him ask of God, who gives to all liberally and without reproach, and it will be given to him" (James 1:5). Wisdom gives us the ability to make right choices in the right way. This is a gift from God. We all need divine wisdom and guidance and we can have the assurance that God will give it to us. Proverbs 11:30b says "And he who wins souls is wise."

CHAPTER 5

THE IMPORTANCE OF PRAYER

Prayer is a practical tool that lets us hear God and receive the wisdom we need to reach others. Praying for people in our private prayer time allows God to show us their needs. We must first recognize that without God's intervention, we cannot effectively minister to others. We must humble ourselves before God and ask Him to show us how to pray for them. God may give you a picture, a Word from the Scriptures, or a sense of how to pray. Praying for others is called *intercessory prayer.* We are bringing the needs of others before God's throne and praying for His perfect will in their lives. Even before we know the specific need, we know that each person can only find fulfillment in God. We can ask God to reveal to the person their need for Him as Lord and Savior. We can pray that God will be glorified through the circumstances. We can pray for His wisdom and timing as to *when* and *how* to share Christ with that individual.

It may be helpful to keep a journal or write down impressions that we sense as God speaks. To ensure accountability in our prayers, it can be helpful to have a prayer partner. At the same time, we need to remember that some information is confidential. General prayer requests for others can be shared without divulging names and secrets.

Through intercessory prayer we enter into the person's suffering. I am not referring to substitution, since only Christ is the substitute for sin. But when we love someone—our children for example—and they are sick, we feel for them. In their illness, we experience grief because we love them. We can also groan and travail for others in their suffering. People who intercede for the lost often weep and cry out to God for their souls. This is called "standing in the gap" (Ezekiel 22:30).

This principle of intercessory prayer became real in my life when my father became seriously ill. He had endured so many strokes that he had lost his speech and vision, and was unable to walk. I loved my father dearly and his agony touched me more deeply than I thought possible. Our whole family felt his suffering. I turned the emotional agony I experienced into prayer for him. In this way I rolled my burden on the Lord. Psalm 55:22 says, "Cast your burden on the Lord, And He shall sustain you; He shall never permit the righteous to be moved."

God doesn't want us to carry these burdens alone. We can bring our troubles to God in prayer and trust Him for His purposes. We do this continually until we receive a breakthrough. God gives us a burden for prayer, so we can give it back to Him, praying with the heart of God for others. This kind of prayer is effective in seeing the hand of God move in a person's life. It also requires great patience because it may take years before we see answers to our prayers. We may even need to receive prayer ourselves, as we minister to others.

I believe that without prayer very little will be accomplished in bringing souls into the kingdom. Prayer is the bedrock spiritual activity for reaching the lost, and may consume more of our time than sharing. Some people are called to pray and find prayer a rewarding and exciting gift to exercise. If you are one of those people, don't be discouraged if you personally don't have many opportunities to pray the sinner's prayer with the lost. Remember there are different gifts and there are different stages in the harvest. Only eternity will reveal how much your prayers accomplished in bringing lost souls into the kingdom of God.

I have found that sharing prayer requests with trusted intercessors has helped me win souls to Jesus Christ. I am grateful for those who have stood with me in praying for others to come to faith. It doesn't negate my own responsibility to pray, but it strengthens me in my ministry.

Praying God's Word

We can have absolute confidence in God's Word because it is true. As we read and study the Bible, we can pray through the verses that pertain to certain situations or people. For example, Jesus tells us to love our enemies and to pray for them (Matthew 5:43–45). A good place to start is to pray for the difficult people in our lives.

When my brother Howard became a Christian, he was in his second year of engineering at the university. He began to share his faith with some of the other students. One student gave Howard a very difficult time, openly mocking and humiliating him in front of the others. Howard began to get upset with this fellow.

One evening as Howard was praying, he felt that he should pray for this student's salvation. He felt reluctant to even think about him let alone pray for him! But Howard felt an insistent urge to pray for his mocker. Howard *chose* to pray for this fellow. That first evening was difficult, but after he prayed for him a couple of nights, he actually enjoyed praying for this student.

About a week later, the student who had bitterly mocked Howard came up to him in the hallway and asked if he could speak to him about God! Howard met with him the next day for half an hour and shared his faith. When Howard had finished sharing with him, the student was convinced of the claims of Christ and gave his heart to Jesus. Today this man pastors a congregation and has a powerful international teaching ministry.

Howard had to pray through the Scriptural command to love your enemy. Howard didn't *feel* like praying for him but he *chose* to pray for him. This was an act of obedience to God's Word. How many opportunities have we missed because we were offended by someone and stopped praying for them? We should pray all the more for those who offend us. This is just one example of how the Scriptures guide us in praying for others.

Sometimes it helps to write out specific Scripture passages that are applicable to the situation. You can then read the Scriptures back to God in a prayerful way, adding your own words of expression. For example in the Lord's Prayer it says, "Your will be done on earth as it is in heaven" (Matthew 6:10). You may pray these words and express them in this way, "Lord you have seen the suffering of this person and I know that Your heart's desire is to see them saved. Use this difficult situation to speak into their life and soften their heart to receive Your salvation." This is an example of seeing the person's earthly condition and seeking God's will and heavenly perspective for them.

You can pray the Scriptures over individuals, groups, and nations in a similar fashion. Recognize the need and commit it to prayer by praying the Scriptures. We know that God is faithful to His Word; so using the Word to pray to God is a powerful way to intercede.

You can also pray the *principles* of the Word. For example, we recognize from the Bible that sometimes God judged the children of Israel when He gave them their request. Psalm 106:15 says, "And He gave them their request, but sent leanness into their soul." Sometimes getting what you want is a judgment rather than a blessing when it is out of the will of God or sought for selfish reasons.

When people get their own way, they often become dissatisfied and unhappy; yet it is this dissatisfaction that makes them seek God. None of the world's possessions or honor will ever satisfy the human heart. When I sense people are caught up in materialism, I pray that they will become dissatisfied with all that the world has to offer and seek the true meaning that only God can bring.

CHAPTER 6

GUIDANCE FROM GOD

Being Led by the Spirit

> Likewise the Spirit also helps in our weaknesses. For we do not know what we should pray for as we ought, but the Spirit Himself makes intercession for us with groanings which cannot be uttered.
>
> —Romans 8:26

Often we don't know how to pray for others. God is the only one who can see into their heart and knows what they truly need, so we need to submit to His leadership and let the Spirit pray through us. We do this through deliberate consecration to God and worship. We don't begin with our need, but with God. As we offer ourselves up to God, He leads us in praying for others and their specific situation. This is what it means to be led by the Spirit in prayer.

As we pray for those who need Christ, amazing things begin to happen. Sometimes God will speak to you about their need, sometimes the person will tell you his or her need. The important thing is to remain sensitive and prayerful.

Romans 8:14 says, "For as many as are led by the Spirit of God, these are sons of God." The word for *sons* means "mature sons" as opposed to children. Being led by the Spirit is a sign of maturity but we are to walk in the Spirit as well (Galatians 5:25). It is important to recognize that the Spirit of God is the One who is orchestrating and guiding our steps in the work of evangelism.

One of the guiding principles in Scripture is to trust God with all your heart, not leaning on your own understanding, but in all your ways acknowledging Him and letting Him direct your path (Proverbs 3:5–6). We must demonstrate faith in God in our own lives before we can preach it to others.

We can have confidence that God will guide us in all our ways. We must trust God and obey Him. The Spirit leaves us with impressions which, if ignored, can lead to disastrous results.

I have often gotten into trouble when I felt a strong sense of restraint and ignored it. I remember a teacher who left the class with a touch of the flu. I felt troubled in my spirit, but I told myself, *It's just the flu!* The next morning we learned that the teacher had passed away during the night from a heart attack. I had overridden the sense of urgency in my spirit by telling myself that this was not a serious matter, when the Spirit of God was trying to get me to intercede for the teacher because he was about to die. It is important to be sensitive to the Spirit's promptings.

On a more positive note, Paul tells us to let the peace of God rule our hearts (Colossians 3:15). When we have a positive sense of God's peace we can proceed. When we have a sense of God's restraint, we stop and wait for either God's timing or for His change of direction. We can trust God to guide us as we wait prayerfully on Him.

How God Guides Us

Here we see how God led Paul, in both a negative sense and a positive sense:

> Now when they had gone through Phrygia and the region of Galatia, they were forbidden by the Holy Spirit to preach the word in Asia. After they had come to Mysia, they tried to go into Bithynia, but the Spirit did not permit them. So passing by Mysia, they came down to Troas. And a vision appeared to Paul in the night. A man of Macedonia stood and pleaded with him, saying, "Come over to Macedonia and help us." Now after he had seen the vision, immediately we sought to go to Macedonia, concluding that the Lord had called us to preach the Gospel to them.
>
> —Acts 16:6–10

The Holy Spirit forbade them to preach the word in Asia, and did not permit them to go to Bithynia. The Holy Spirit was leading them, actively directing the course of their lives. We can have that same confidence that God will guide our lives.

God closed one door, but He opened another one. The text doesn't tell us *why*. The important thing is that Paul obeyed the Holy Spirit. He didn't argue with God. He didn't ask why he needed to be in Asia or suggest that God send someone else to Macedonia. It says, "Now after he had seen the vision, immediately we sought to go to Macedonia, concluding that the Lord had called us to preach the Gospel to them."

We may have our own ideas about how the Gospel should be preached and to whom, but the Lord knows best. I have heard that someone went to Abraham Lincoln during the Civil War and asked him, "Whose side is God on, the North or the South?" Abraham Lincoln replied, "Sir, my concern is not whether God is on our side; my greatest concern is to be on God's side, for God is always right." We would be more effective if we spent time waiting for God's plan, which will already be blessed, than producing a flurry of activity for God.

At our church, the pastor and elders take all of my proposed evangelism programs before the Lord for His direction. This helps me personally because it makes me accountable and provides the checks and balances I need for effective ministry. When the elders don't sense God's leading in a certain direction, I am not offended because it is not my agenda; it is God's, and He will open another door if this is not the path I am to take. We can have confidence that God will lead us. He wants to see the lost saved even more than we do. He has a plan and you are a part of it!

Before we move on to the next section, let me share a few practical tips. As a general practice, it is best for men to share the Gospel with men, women with women, and children with children. The enemy often complicates matters when gender lines are crossed. The message can get mixed, and cause difficulties that could have been avoided. This is not to make a hard and fast rule, but it is important to be aware of the dangers.

My wife and I often work together as a team in sharing the Gospel. We will invite another couple to our home, or out for an event, so we can get to know them personally. Invariably, at some point we have an opportunity to share our faith in a natural, relaxed way. This often leads to more times together.

God has used our children to share the Gospel with others, too. When my daughter Jessica was six years old, she became best friends with another little girl in her class. Her friend's father was a teacher at a school they both attended. For several months, Jessica wanted the two families to get together. One Saturday in March, Jessica got the other little girl's father on the phone and talked me into inviting them to join us at the Sugar Bush, an annual event in our area where syrup is harvested from maple trees. They sell pancakes and maple syrup and you can ride a horse-drawn carriage into the woods where there are demonstrations of how the early settlers gathered sap to produce maple syrup.

We spent the day at the Sugar Bush with Kevin and Sharon and their two children. At the time, the school was in an uproar over an issue involving the principal. Parents were divided. Marriages dissolved. Friendships ended. Kevin was right in the thick of the conflict and at odds with the principal. This dispute eventually led to the principal's dismissal and a split in the school, but at that time it was still unresolved.

We were at the Sugar Bush with this couple and their children right at the height of the tension—*and I was avoiding the subject like the plague!* Kevin was dying to know where I stood, so he asked me, "Harvey, what do you think about the problem at school?" I told him that I knew exactly what was going on and left it at that. He replied, "You do? Could you please tell me?" I told him that the Bible says that men will fall in one of three areas: sex, money and power. The Apostle John calls them the lust of the flesh, the lust of the eyes, and the pride of life (1 John 2:16).

Kevin was stunned. He had not realized that the Bible was relevant to the situation and this led to a discussion about the Bible. Later that day as we were having a treat at the Dairy Queen, I brought out my Bible and we talked some more.

A few days later, Diane met Sharon at the school. Sharon wanted to know if they could talk about the Bible, because she had questions. *Mind?* Not only did we not mind, we were thrilled! Under the right circumstances it is surprising how eager people are to talk about spiritual things.

Several weeks later, in May, we invited them over to celebrate Victoria Day. That morning I had had a dream. I dreamt that a mother eagle was looking down at a baby eagle. One word came to me in the dream, "imprinting." Imprinting is a natural phenomenon where the baby bird's identity is established by gazing at the mother bird during the first few days of its young life. The baby eagle knows it's an eagle because of this imprinting.

While I was coming out of sleep, a Scripture verse from 2 Corinthians 3:18 came to my mind: "But we all, with unveiled face, beholding as in a mirror the glory of the Lord, are being transformed into the same image from glory to glory, just as by the Spirit of the Lord."

We are recreated into the image of Jesus Christ at the new birth. I thought about the dream and the verse, then said to Diane, "I think that we need to present the right picture of Jesus to them so they can experience the "new birth."

Later that day, they came to our home for a barbecue. After lunch we again spoke about spiritual matters. I told them how to receive Jesus as their Lord and Savior and asked them if they wanted to pray with me to receive Him by faith. Sharon with slight hesitation said, "I cannot speak for Kevin" At that moment I thought she would say no, but to my surprise she continued, "but I would like to!" Kevin immediately said to me, "I would like to as well." Right there, Kevin and Sharon prayed a prayer of faith and repentance and gave their lives to Jesus Christ.

Later that day we went for a walk in a park and Sharon asked, "Does God speak through signs?" It was a good question. I told her that Jesus warned us that an adulterous generation seeks a sign (Matthew 12:39) but that signs and wonders follow those who believe (Mark 16:17). In other words, we are to seek God and not signs, but God often confirms His Word through signs and wonders.

A few minutes later we stopped by a swing and noticed that there was a little stirring in the crotch of the frame. When we looked we found a nest with two newly hatched baby birds. At that moment I didn't think that this was a sign for Kevin and Sharon. They had only been born again for a few hours but I felt that it was a sign for me, confirming my dream from earlier that morning! Later that week I shared the dream and my insight with them and they were very encouraged.

A couple of weeks later Kevin shared with me that a year earlier he had had two dreams. In the first dream he was lost in a mall and the mall was closing. No one was around and he felt disoriented and afraid. He tried to run but got nowhere. Suddenly the mall owner came and took him by the arm and led him to his family waiting outside in their blue Hyundai. Then they followed the mall owner in his white minivan. The mall owner's wife was directing them with her arm out the window.

Our family owns a small mall and at the time we owned a white minivan. I felt that the dream was a picture of how Kevin had lost his way in life, but God was preparing him for salvation. When they first met us, they followed us to the Sugar Bush in our white van while Diane directed them with her arm out of the window!

Kevin had a second dream while he was working at the school. In his dream he was sitting in the hallway on a blue chair and I was sitting next to him. The principal's office door was open and through the open door he could see the principal in his office. I was telling him what the principal had given him and what he had given the principal. The interesting thing is that I had not yet met Kevin!

God gave us the interpretation to the dream. Kevin sitting in the hallway represented his falling out of favor with the principal. The conflict with the principal had drawn Kevin to Jesus. When Kevin became a Christian, he forgave the principal and began to pray for him.

Before we even met, God was preparing Kevin and Sharon's hearts. I had the privilege of sharing the Gospel with them but it was the Holy Spirit who had prepared their hearts to receive Jesus. A year later, Kevin, Sharon, their daughter Amanda, and our daughter Jessica were baptized in water. I remember Kevin thanking God for Jessica, because through her witness—and I might add her persistence—the Knell family came into the kingdom of God.

Only the Spirit Can Reveal Jesus

Only the Spirit can prepare the hearts of those called to salvation. We are not to play "Junior Holy Spirit." He does the job perfectly without our help. When Jesus asked His disciples who men said that He was, they gave many different answers—not one of which was correct! But when Jesus asked His disciples who they said that He was, Peter replied that He was the Messiah, the Son of the Living God (Matthew 16:16). Then Jesus replied, "flesh and blood did not reveal this to you but My Father in Heaven."

Believing in Jesus must be a work of the Spirit and is not deduced by natural methods alone. This accomplishes two things: it forces us to depend on the Holy Spirit to reveal Christ to others and it relieves us of the responsibility of convincing people of their need. No amount of arguing will convince anyone of anything. Prayer and trusting God for the salvation of others will accomplish much.

A friend of mine put it this way, "When we work, God rests and when we rest, God works." Rest is not the absence of activity but ceasing from self-effort. Results are God's business, and obedience is our business. Let God speak to the hearts of others as we rest in God's provision.

CHAPTER 7

PERSONAL SPACE AND THE SPIRITUAL BAROMETER

Respecting Personal Space

People do not like others to cross their boundaries. We should always keep this in mind when we are sharing the Gospel. A friendly greeting is appropriate with a friend, but pulling a stranger into a big bear hug is not. The better we get to know someone, the more they will let us into their personal space. In the same way, people have spiritual boundaries. It takes time and trust before people will let us know their deep hopes and fears.

Trust must be earned. It is important to be sensitive and watch for cues. If you violate someone's space, they probably won't smash a baseball bat over your head, but they will signal their discomfort in other ways.

In a new relationship, people will set boundaries fairly quickly. I often start by mentioning church or other impersonal Christian activities, such as a neighborhood Bible Study, and see how they respond. If they don't ask questions or show any interest, I say no more. If they are curious about my beliefs, I simply respond to their questions. If I ask something and they change the subject, then I know that they are not ready.

You can also ask gentle questions, being careful not to get too personal too quickly. Try not to ask too many questions that are closed ended, and can be answered with a simple "Yes" or "No." Instead ask open-ended questions that will make people think and give them an opportunity to share, such as, *What evidence for God do you see in the world? Why does suffering make it so difficult to believe in God? How can we explain a loving God in a world of injustice?* These questions are not personal; they won't make a person feel vulnerable or judged. They simply allow them to express what they think about the issues of life.

As you get to know people and they begin to trust you, they will let you into their personal space and share more openly. They may even share needs. Then you can ask if they would like you to pray for their needs. If they say "No," don't press them. *But they may say, "Yes!"*

To illustrate this principle, I like the story of Queen Esther and King Ahasuerus. Queen Ester was not allowed to go before the King uninvited. If she did, she would be killed unless the king held out his scepter to her. If he didn't, she would lose her life (Esther 5:2). Esther appeared before the King only after much spiritual preparation, and he graciously extended the scepter to her. He was delighted to do so because she had won his heart.

As we win the favor of those with whom we share the Gospel, we can have confidence that we can "knock" on the door of their heart and be granted access to their personal space. Each person is different. Some people like Kevin and Sharon opened up to us quickly; others can take a couple of years, and still others have yet to open up. When we knock on the doors of their lives, we must wait for them to extend an invitation before we come in. We should not barge into people's lives uninvited, but let them set the boundaries. Knocking is simply asking permission to enter; it is not invading their space.

Reading the Spiritual Barometer

A barometer is an instrument used to determine atmospheric pressure, to assist in forecasting weather, and to determine altitude.[1] Just as "personal space" defines how close we can get to people, their "spiritual barometer" indicates how close they are to God. When I use the term "barometer" in a metaphorical context, I am referring to a person's degree of spiritual interest. Are they hot or cold toward the Gospel? Have they expressed an interest in Jesus Christ? This is important because if we know people's heart toward God, our prayers and witness will be more effective.

In the parable of the sower, Jesus depicts four kinds of people that we will meet when we share the Gospel of Jesus Christ.

> Then He spoke many things to them in parables, saying: "Behold, a sower went out to sow. And as he sowed, some seed fell by the wayside; and the birds came and devoured them. Some fell on stony places, where they did not have much earth; and they immediately sprang up because they had no depth of earth. But when the sun was up they were scorched, and because they had no root they withered away. And some fell among thorns, and the thorns sprang up and choked them. But others fell on good ground and yielded a crop: some a hundredfold, some sixty, some thirty. He who has ears to hear, let him hear!"

And the disciples came and said to Him, "Why do You speak to them in parables?"

He answered and said to them, "Because it has been given to you to know the mysteries of the kingdom of heaven, but to them it has not been given. For whoever has, to him more will be given, and he will have abundance; but whoever does not have, even what he has will be taken away from him. Therefore I speak to them in parables, because seeing they do not see, and hearing they do not hear, nor do they understand. And in them the prophecy of Isaiah is fulfilled, which says:

'Hearing you will hear and shall not understand, And seeing you will see and not perceive; For the hearts of this people have grown dull. Their ears are hard of hearing, And their eyes they have closed, Lest they should see with their eyes and hear with their ears, Lest they should understand with their hearts and turn, So that I should heal them.'

But blessed are your eyes for they see, and your ears for they hear; for assuredly, I say to you that many prophets and righteous men desired to see what you see, and did not see it, and to hear what you hear, and did not hear it.

Therefore hear the parable of the sower: When anyone hears the word of the kingdom, and does not understand it, then the wicked one comes and snatches away what was sown in his heart. This is he who received seed by the wayside. But he who received the seed on stony places, this is he who hears the word and immediately receives it with joy; yet he has no root in himself, but endures only for a while. For when tribulation or persecution arises because of the word, immediately

> he stumbles. Now he who received seed among the thorns is he who hears the word, and the cares of this world and the deceitfulness of riches choke the word, and he becomes unfruitful. But he who received seed on the good ground is he who hears the word and understands it, who indeed bears fruit and produces: some a hundredfold, some sixty, some thirty."
> —Matthew 13:3–23

Here is a rough gauge to determine a person's level of spiritual interest:

1) The Unconvinced are people we would normally refer to as *unbelievers*. They are simply not interested in the Gospel of Jesus Christ. Their hearts are filled with unbelief and they don't understand the message. They are like the soil that is by the wayside, where it does not take root. It is important to accept these people with unconditional love and to pray that God will show them their spiritual needs and change their hearts. It is wrong to pressure anyone, but we should be especially careful to not pressure these people. Applying pressure will turn them off and may make them even more determined to resist. Allow God to do the work that you cannot accomplish.

The "unconvinced" are not necessarily going to reject Jesus, but they certainly are not going to accept Him at this time, in their present state of life. But God has a way of changing the "soil conditions" of the heart. A friend of ours prayed for her parents' salvation for years. They were hard-working immigrants who were raised in a strong religious tradition of "good works." They were very upset when their daughter gave her heart to Jesus.

She was afraid they would never receive Christ, and she couldn't mention the Gospel without a battle. Several years ago, her father became ill with cancer. He became fearful about death and aware of his own sinfulness. He knew he wasn't prepared to die and meet God. When Diane and I went to visit him, he was glad to see us and we had a warm visit. I asked if I could share with him a special message of hope for his difficult situation. He agreed and I shared salvation through faith in Jesus Christ. I asked him if we could pray together, and he agreed and received Jesus. In fact, he and his wife both prayed to receive the Lord! This is just one example of how God can take the seed that was sown on the wayside and change the "soil conditions" of the heart. He eventually died—physically—*but he is alive eternally!*

2) Inquirers have an interest in the Gospel but no commitment. There are two types of people in this category.

The first category of inquirers includes people who are like the seed sown in the stony places. They like to come to church and hear the music and listen to a good sermon, but their lives are virtually unaffected by the message of repentance and faith. Someone once described such individuals as being interested in the Gospel versus making a commitment to it. Think about a breakfast of bacon and eggs, the chicken has an interest in the breakfast, *but the pig is committed!* Those with a passing interest are not hostile to the Gospel but when difficulties arise, the true nature of their heart is revealed. They are unwilling to go on with God. Their interest is passive and not active.

We had a Jewish friend who was initially antagonistic to the Gospel, but who eventually surrendered his heart to Jesus. For the first year of his new-found faith he was growing spiritually and was passionate about God. Then a crisis came and he had to decide if he would continue to follow Jesus and suffer rejection from his family, or abandon his new-found faith. He decided that the cost was too great, and he turned away. This is a classic example of seed sown among the stony places.

The second category includes inquirers who are like the seeds scattered among the thorns. Jesus said that the thorns represent the cares of this world and the deceitfulness of riches. These things choke out the Word in their lives and they become unfruitful. I have seen this happen all too often, as people become distracted. Life's pressures will cause us to draw closer to God or to pull away from Him. I have seen more people backslide because of the cares of the world and the deceitfulness of riches than for any other reason. I have friends who showed a real interest in the Gospel and came very close to accepting Jesus, but put it off and eventually lost interest because the pressures and pleasures of life grabbed their attention.

Christians also need to be careful not to fall into this trap. Someone once told me that if you put a frog in boiling water it will jump out quickly because of the dramatic change of temperature, but if you put it in cool water and raise the temperature gradually, it will not notice the incremental change and will boil to death! The latter describes people who start off on the right path but veer off. They change course in small degrees until one day they are no longer following Jesus. They start well but become too busy for prayer or devotions. Then they skip church once in a while and soon they are not in fellowship with God or other believers and have lost their spiritual passion. The gardens of our hearts need to be weeded daily by confessing and forsaking sin and walking with God through prayer and Bible study.

Paul met some inquirers at Mars Hill.

> And they took him and brought him to the Areopagus, saying, "May we know what this new doctrine is of which you speak? For you are bringing some strange things to our ears. There-

> fore we want to know what these things mean." For all the Athenians and the foreigners who were there spent their time in nothing else but either to tell or to hear some new thing.
> —Acts 17:19–21

Paul used that opportunity to share his faith in Christ. They were willing to hear what he had to say. The inquirers are different from the unconvinced who don't want to hear what you have to say. This group is not antagonistic, but has only a passing interest in the Gospel. You may share with them if they are willing to listen, and then pray that God will fuel their passion for Him. Paul received a mixed response at Mars Hill. Some believed, some mocked, and some were willing to listen further (Acts 17:32–34).

3) Seekers are people who have more than a passing interest in the Gospel; they are looking for the truth. At this stage of their walk they are probably going to church, Bible study, or Alpha. They may be reading the Bible or other Christian books, but may not have enough information to make a decision. The seed is planted in good ground, but has not yet sprung up to produce a harvest.

A seeker can be recognized by the questions they ask. I remember one Jewish person who asked me, "Can I still be Jewish and believe in Jesus?" When someone asks a question like that, they are thinking about following Jesus. Often people ask questions about the cost of the decision to follow Christ and the changes that will follow. Receiving Jesus is a major decision! The cost may be high, especially in countries or cultures where a believer may lose his life for believing.

Many people are afraid to give up control. They see the benefits of salvation, but they also see the price. Jesus told His disciples to count the cost. We need to let people understand the price they will have to pay so they can make an informed decision. The gift of eternal life in Christ is absolutely free—there is nothing anyone can do to earn it, but following Jesus will cost everything. Once we receive the gift of eternal life, we need to be whole-hearted followers of Christ.

Seekers are gathering information so they can understand the decision they are making and the price of following Jesus. Salvation is more than "fire insurance;" it is a radical inward transformation into a new life created in the image of Jesus. We must be careful not to create "religious hoops" that people must jump through to come to Christ. If we give people a long list of do's and don'ts that they must sign off on before they can give their lives to Jesus, we risk making salvation dependent on our good deeds and not on heartfelt surrender to God.

I have a friend who was pro-abortion when she came to faith. Once she gave her life to Jesus, God changed her heart toward the unborn. I am thankful that no one made her views on abortion a condition for her salvation.

The act of becoming a Christian is very easy, but the implications are profound. Some people refuse to come to Christ because they are afraid they will have to stand on a street corner wearing a sandwich board that reads "Repent! The end is near!" Or that they will have to go to Africa and live in a mud hut or have to stay single all of their life. These are just a few of the crazy notions that keep people from finding Christ. What we must communicate is that God will fill their life with wonderful purpose and they will become exactly who God created them to be (Ephesians 2:8–10).

Although it is hard to give up control of our lives, we all need to understand that we are happiest when we are in the will of God.

Just like our ancestors in the Garden of Eden, our natural tendency is to want to be like God (Genesis 3:5). There is a cost to following Jesus, but we must emphasize that the benefits far outweigh the price. God's character can be trusted and He knows what is best for our lives.

This wonderful promise of Scripture comes from Jeremiah 29:13: "And you will seek Me and find Me, when you search for Me with all your heart."

4) Finders have found God. He has promised in His Word that those who seek *will find!* The experience and thrill of knowing God cannot be expressed in words. We can *know* God! A sense of urgency is inherent in genuine seeking: when you are looking for something, you are troubled until you find it.

Finders are really seekers who, after making an informed decision, have decided to follow Jesus. This is the seed sown into good ground. Jesus describes them this way, "But he who received seed on the good ground is **he who hears the word and understands it**, who indeed bears fruit and produces: some a hundredfold, some sixty, some thirty" (Matthew 13:8).

One of the strange paradoxes of the Christian life is that when you find God, you still keep seeking Him. It is difficult to describe. Once I found Jesus, I wanted more of Him. A friend told me that one of the secrets of the Christian life is to stay hungry. It is like finding a mansion with many rooms—you want to explore it and see all the rooms. The mystery of God is not settled when you come to faith. It is only the beginning. The best place to start is in His Word, the Bible, for it is a "mansion" with many rooms.

We never want to stop being a seeker. We seek, and then we find, and then we seek again. This is the mystery of God and the mystery of His will, knowing and loving Him, more and more and more. Hallelujah!

Some people, on coming to Christ, believe they have arrived. This is true in one sense, but in another sense it is only the beginning. That is why I would add another category: Keepers.

5) Keepers are individuals who come to faith, then pursue a full life in Christ. Our salvation is fixed at the point in time where we first made our decision, but it is also an ongoing process. We are saved, but we are also still being saved. The continuing work of salvation is called "sanctification." Paul tells us to work out our salvation with fear and trembling (Philippians 2:12). Oswald Chambers says, "We work out our salvation, not for it." What God has worked into us by His Spirit needs to be applied to our lives each day.

This means that we must grow continually in the faith or we will fall back—*there is no middle ground!* We are in a constant state of movement, either toward God or away from Him. At the moment of salvation God redeemed us for His good purpose, but it is our responsibility to continue to abide in Him, by faith, with obedience. In this way we see His purposes fulfilled.

Now we have a heavenly point of view. We must pray and ask God for His direction for our lives and not just do as we please. Our choices will change. Our values will change. Our attitudes will change. We take on the nature and character of Jesus in our everyday lives. We love God first and foremost, and then love others. Our selfishness is put to death, so that now we *want* to look out for other people.

As we continue in this new life, we grow. Spiritual fruit is the result of an intimate relationship with God through Jesus Christ (John 15), a changed character (Galatians 5:22–23), and a life of good works (James 2:26).

Understanding the Relationship Between Personal Space and the Spiritual Barometer

When we first get to know people, and we are exploring where they are in their relationship with God, we must remain sensitive to how they are responding. Even though I have used a scientific term, barometer, to describe this relationship, relationships between people and God do not follow cut and dried scientific formulas. Relationships are complex and not easily defined. We need first to cultivate relationships, making small adjustments as they develop. As we get to know people, we will sense what is appropriate by reading their social cues and body language. If they appear awkward or uncomfortable, I try to determine if it is something I have said or something else. We adjust our approach to be in tune with their response, so they do not feel threatened or pressured. We don't want to rush them.

Several years ago, I shared my faith with some friends who showed some real interest. I was thrilled! In fact, they left my house with their arms piled high with books. A couple of days later, I received a shipment from a courier company. All of my books were in the box, with a little note thanking me and saying that they were not interested. My enthusiasm had overwhelmed them, turning them off. Thankfully the relationship survived, but it was a powerful lesson. Now I let them bring up matters of faith, and they are again asking questions and listening to my stories once again.

When we share our faith, we have to stay sensitive to the other person's spiritual barometer (where they are with God) and their personal space (where they are with us). We must establish healthy, loving relationships with people outside the faith. We need to take time to understand where they are with God so we know how to pray for them and how to speak into their lives. This leads us to the second theme of this series, *You are a Life Message.*

PART 2

PREPARATION: *You Are A Life Message*

> The voice of one crying in the wilderness:
> "Prepare the way of the LORD;
> Make straight in the desert
> A highway for our God.
> Every valley shall be exalted
> And every mountain and hill brought low;
> The crooked places shall be made straight
> And the rough places smooth;
> The glory of the Lord shall be revealed,
> And all flesh shall see it together;
> For the mouth of the Lord has spoken."
> —Isaiah 40:3–5

The importance of building godly character and being empowered by the Holy Spirit cannot be overstated. We need both to be ready to effectively share the Gospel.

Many years ago, I sensed that the Lord was speaking to my heart saying that I was not to look for a ministry, but to look for Him. It doesn't mean that I am idle or indifferent. It means that as my life in God deepens, I am being prepared for the doors which He will open for me to serve Him. I don't have to maneuver myself into the right ministry or compete with others for a choice spot. I simply have to look for Him. Ever since I began doing this, He has opened many doors to fulfilling ministry.

There is no real ministry unless Christ is central in our lives. It requires a daily consecration and surrender to the purposes of God. In this section I want to focus on this point: what God does *in* you is more important than what God does *through* you. What God does in you is your business. What God does through you is His business. We often take the opposite attitude, leaving God out of our business and trying to tell Him how He should conduct His business.

To put it another way, obedience to God is our responsibility; the results of our obedience are His responsibility. We can take no credit for great results and need not accept blame for poor results. Success is measured by how we have served God, not by what we have accomplished. There is no basis for prideful achievement, only gratitude that God chose to use us at all.

God wants each of us to be a life message, but before this can happen we must let God prepare us. The first part of our preparation happens when we repent from running our own life. The second part happens when we let God mold our character so that we have the character of Christ. The third part happens as Jesus Christ is revealed in our lives to others.

CHAPTER 8

REPENTANCE AND PREPARATION

> There was a man sent from God, whose name was John. This man came for a witness, to bear witness of the Light; that all through him might believe. He was not that Light, but was sent to bear witness of that Light.
>
> —John 1:6–8

Living life in the fast lane can burn us out and tangle our priorities. God sometimes allows seasons of trial to slow us down and show us what is important in our lives. In this section we see the priority God places on godly character and how suffering can draw us to Him and bring forth His work in our lives. John the Baptist was indeed a good example of "a voice crying in the wilderness." Just as John prepared the way of the Lord, God also can use us to prepare the way for others.

Our lives are to be a witness for Christ. There is nothing more appealing than the presence of Jesus shining out of the life of a believer who is walking in the light. A believer who radiates the character of Christ—love, joy, peace, patience, compassion—naturally draws people to Jesus. Where do we begin? Like John the Baptist in

John 1:6–7, we can bear witness to the Light as we live our lives and share our faith.

Who was John? John said, "I am '*The voice of one crying in the wilderness: "Make straight the way of the* LORD,'" as the prophet Isaiah said" (John 1:23). John was the forerunner of the Messiah, a prestigious position if ever there was one, but he described himself only as a "voice crying in the wilderness." His entire ministry was to "prepare the way of the Lord"—to prepare the people for the coming Messiah.

What did Jesus say about John? Jesus told the multitudes, in Matthew 11:9, that John was "*more than a prophet.*" More than a prophet! This period in history is often referred to as the silent years, because for four hundred years there were no prophets in Israel. No wonder the people were so curious about John!

Jesus also said that "among those born of women there has not risen one greater than John the Baptist." This is an extraordinary statement. If one were to think of the greatest prophets of all time, we might think of Abraham, the father of our faith. We might think of Moses, the law giver whom God used to deliver the children of Israel out of Egypt. Perhaps Elijah would be at the top of our list, as he called down fire from heaven that consumed the burnt offering!

John the Baptist was greater than all of them! John did no miracles during his ministry (John 10:41), and yet Jesus said he was the greatest. Why? Because Jesus says, "all the prophets and the law prophesied until John" (Matthew 11:13). John the Baptist was the greatest not because of who he was but because of whom he prepared the way for—Jesus.

From Genesis forward, all the prophets and the law point to Christ. Jesus Christ is the center of God's purposes for all time and eternity. I remember hearing many years ago that history is *His Story.*

The law and the prophets had only a vague and shadowy understanding of the significance and fullness of Christ. First Peter 1:10–12 says, "Of this salvation the prophets have inquired and searched carefully, who prophesied of the grace that would come to you." They inquired. They searched carefully to see the coming Messiah. And Messiah came . . . in the person of Jesus!

Jesus Christ is the most important person in all of history. The law and the prophets predicted His coming; but John the Baptist was the one who announced His coming in person! Truly John was the greatest prophet of all until the coming of Jesus.

Jesus then introduced another enigma; "but he who is least in the kingdom of heaven is greater than he" (Matthew 11:11). That last "he" refers to John the Baptist. What did Jesus mean? John the Baptist was the greatest prophet and now we read that those who are least in the kingdom of heaven are greater than John. John was able to point to Christ and tell the people, "Here He is, the One you have been waiting for!" But John was not able to tell the whole story. He didn't know about the cross. He didn't know that salvation would be available to all mankind.

Anyone who has accepted Jesus as Savior knows the full story of redemption—salvation through faith in Jesus Christ because of His life, death and resurrection. In other words, even the newest believer, who has just accepted Jesus, is greater than John the Baptist, because even the "least in the kingdom" knows the Gospel message. John was still under the Old Covenant but we are under the New Covenant. We are not greater because of who we are, but because of our message and our relationship with Christ.

John did not experience the new birth, because Jesus had not yet gone to the cross. As believers in Jesus we *enjoy* and *experience* the new birth. We receive a new nature, the nature of Jesus Christ (2 Corinthians 5:17).

If John the Baptist had a motto it would probably be John 3:30: "He must increase but I must decrease." This is also true for us as believers in Jesus Christ. He must be in the driver's seat, while we take a back seat. This is what we call *lordship*. If Jesus Christ is Lord, then we are His servants. He calls the shots. Our job is to be obedient to the revealed will of God. Obviously we cannot be obedient in ignorance. Paul exhorted us not to be ignorant, but to know God's will for our lives (Ephesians 5:17). In praying for the believers in Colosse, Paul stated, "we have not stopped praying for you, and asking God to fill you with the knowledge of His will" (Colossians 1:9).

John was a man with a mission and a message. His mission was to prepare the hearts of the people for the coming Messiah. His message was for people to repent, for the kingdom of God was at hand (Matthew 3:2). Without repentance we miss out on what God is doing.

John the Baptist's message was *repent*! Not just for sinful deeds, but for sinful self. We all want our own way. As Christians we need to repent daily and take up our cross and follow Him. It is a lifestyle of repentance—more than turning away from sinful deeds, the fruit of selfishness. We don't just confess when we are aware of specific sins, but trust in Christ moment-by-moment, being committed to setting aside our interests so that His life can be manifested in us.

The Hebrew word *repent* means "to return." We must turn from serving ourselves to serving God. When the Spirit of God convicts us of a wrong attitude, we turn to God and away from sin. We confess our sin and turn away from it, trusting the Spirit of Christ within us to overcome sin by His power.

If we want to be effective witnesses for Christ, we cannot do it alone; it must be Christ in us. We need to understand that self-effort cannot accomplish God's work. Unless obedience to His Spirit is accomplished through grace, our struggle is futile. It comes back to simple trust and obedience. As He increases, we decrease by putting our selfish ambition to death. We must become nothing in ourselves, so that He can become everything in us.

The Greek word *repentance* means "to change one's mind." We must choose to think thoughts that please God rather than our own thoughts (Philippians 4:8). This is accomplished by renewing our mind as we let God expose the lies we believe and replace them with His truth (Romans 12:1–2). God gives us grace as we trust Him for His strength to overcome sin. He has already given us everything we need to live a godly life (2 Peter 1:3).

I mention this because without a holy life no one will see the Lord (Hebrews 12:14). We want others to see Christ in us so they will be drawn to Him. If we lack the reality of God in our lives we become ineffective tools for His kingdom.

We are not talking about being perfect. We are talking about being on the right path, headed in the right direction. We will fail since we all have shortcomings. But if we sincerely desire to follow Christ, God will use us. It is in our poverty of soul that God does some of His best work. He uses our weakness to bring glory to Himself.

> And He said to me, "My grace is sufficient for you, for My strength is made perfect in weakness." Therefore most gladly I will rather boast in my infirmities, that the power of Christ may rest upon me. Therefore I take pleasure in infirmities, in reproaches, in

> needs, in persecutions, in distresses, for Christ's sake. For when I am weak, then I am strong.
>
> —2 Corinthians 12:9–10

It is easy to be afraid of where repentance and obedience may take us. Jesus asked the crowd who had come to see John, "What were you expecting to see? A reed shaken by the wind?" In other words, did they expect to find an unstable or crazy man who claimed to be a prophet?

That is a good question. We often stereotype men of God as "a little on the crazy side." A reed shaken by the wind bends in whatever direction the wind blows. There are dozens of examples of sincere believers who have damaged God's kingdom by their weird behavior. This is not to judge them; it is simply a fact. Many people have been turned off to the Gospel by unstable believers.

Some have even said that about me. I remember one person who said, "I could never become a Christian; I could never live like you!" He was afraid that becoming a Christian would change him into someone other than himself.

When my brother-in-law came to faith in Christ, his parents worried that he was going to wear a sandwich board and stand on downtown street corners telling people that the end was near. People often worry that they will have to become missionaries, or live in monasteries for the rest of their lives. It is true that God *may* call some to unusual ministries, but this is not the norm.

The Alpha Course is a series of ten videotapes that address questions about the Christian faith. On one of the videos, Nicky Gumbel, the Alpha Chaplain says, "God wants you to be normal, and that might come as a relief to some of you." In fact it did come as a relief to many in our group watching the video.

People are afraid that coming to Christ may turn them into people like those depicted in *Invasion of the Body Snatchers*, a fictional movie about people whose bodies were taken over by aliens from outer space. People are afraid if they give their lives to Christ that they will lose their personality and some entity will take over and turn them into zombies or something worse! The exact opposite is true. You will become who you were meant to be; you become fully human—the person God always intended.

Jesus went to the other extreme and asked the crowd if they expected to see "a man clothed in soft clothing?" Jesus then answered His own question by saying, "No, those who wear soft clothing are in king's houses." This was an intentional barb against the Jewish leaders because John was not in the king's palace—but in prison—and not in soft clothing. He was suffering for the sake of the truth, and was, as we know, eventually beheaded.

Many people believe that becoming a Christian is a formula for success. Here Jesus paints quite a different picture. There is a cost to following the call of God.

God wants to bless us. Every blessing we receive comes from Him. But that does not guarantee a pain-free life. We have to make sacrifices on our walk of faith. I believe there is suffering in life regardless of whether or not one follows Christ. We are responsible for some of our suffering and some is caused by the actions and choices of others. Romans 8:28 says that when we suffer according to the will of God, He uses it for His glory and to our benefit.

If we trust Jesus and cling to Him in times of suffering, He will transform us. Remember, you are a life message! I have been amazed at the number of people who have told me, "I've been watching you."

They scrutinize me when they know I am suffering. God uses our failures and frailties to conform us to the image of Jesus Christ. This is what the prophet meant when he announced, "Prepare the way of the Lord."

Suffering purifies what God has already put within us by His grace. Suffering doesn't earn us brownie points toward heaven. The opposite is true: our acceptance into heaven makes us worthy to suffer for His sake.

CHAPTER 9

LESSONS IN THE DESERT: DEVELOPING GODLY CHARACTER

> The voice of one crying in the wilderness:
> "Prepare the way of the Lord;
> Make straight in the desert
> A highway for our God.
> Every valley shall be exalted
> And every mountain and hill brought low;
> The crooked places shall be made straight."
> —Isaiah 40:3–4

A voice is crying in the wilderness. The wilderness sounds like a strange place to proclaim a message of salvation, doesn't it? It is filled with snakes, jackals, rocks and cactuses—and little else. So, what does the wilderness represent? What can we learn from the wilderness?

The wilderness is best understood when we think about where this Scripture was written—in the Middle East where the wilderness is a desolate place with no water, little vegetation, and little life. The natural habitat includes poisonous snakes and scorpions. A person would die very quickly in this environment without fresh water and food. It is incredibly hot—sometimes unbearably so. Indeed, shelter from the oppressive heat of the day is absolutely essential.

God brought the children of Israel out of Egypt into the wilderness to prepare them for the Promised Land. In the wilderness we come to the end of our human strength and must depend upon God's strength. The wilderness may not be a physical place but it will certainly be a spiritual place. There are no shortcuts.

God brings us into the wilderness to teach us His ways so that we will depend on Him. It is interesting that the word for *wilderness* in Hebrew, (midbar), has the same root letters as the word for *speaking*, (davar). It was in the wilderness that God spoke to the children of Israel and told them that man cannot live by bread alone but by every word that proceeds from the mouth of God (Deuteronomy 8:3). God often speaks to us in the wilderness. When things are going well in our life, we don't need God and don't have time for Him. So God takes us on a little "wilderness" journey to spend some time with Him and to develop a relationship of dependency.

Your wilderness may be different from mine. Yours may be a financial wilderness filled with desperate financial needs. Or it may be a spiritual desert where you feel forsaken by God. I have met many believers who had a honeymoon experience with God when they first came to faith. Shortly afterward, it seemed as if God was a million miles away. He was there, but perhaps taking them through a wilderness experience.

God uses different problems and struggles to get our attention. His purpose is always for our good, and we should never doubt that. He is training us or untraining us, as the case may be—we have so many bad habits and sinful ways! God uses the wilderness to expose us, so we can see what is really there beneath the thin veneer of having it all together. In the wilderness we overcome the flesh, which can become a testimony that demonstrates the grace of God to others. As we continue to trust God, He transforms us from within so that His life is outwardly expressed through us.

Our "life message" is often born out of weakness—not strength. Think of Abraham who was childless, yet was called by God the "father of many nations" (Genesis 17:5). God used Abraham's weakness to fulfill His promise. Think of David, the youngest of Jesse's sons, who tended the sheep and was called by God to shepherd His people, Israel. God often takes the broken and shameful places in our lives and heals us so that we can be used to heal others. In this way, our life story becomes a message of hope to a hurting world.

Who is better equipped to reach drug addicts than one who was once enslaved? What about alcoholism or other besetting sins? We are not limited to sharing with those who are going through similar struggles, but sharing how Christ set us free is powerful. Those who have experienced the power of Christ setting them free have an effective testimony—even to those who are not addicted.

It is awesome to hear a powerful testimony! Through our struggles and suffering, God is shaping our lives into His message. He works in us through the trials we face, never leaving or forsaking us. It is not the trials that change us; it is the power of God. The trials merely *reveal the need.* And if we don't respond in obedience to the Spirit of God during the trial, then we will find ourselves in the wilderness once again, until we do. We would do well to remember that, of their entire generation, only Joshua and Caleb entered the Promised Land!

Going through a trial will not guarantee spiritual maturity, but it will demonstrate God's faithfulness to us. He will always be faithful, but the question is *will we trust Him enough to let Him to have His way?*

It is reassuring to know that as we submit to God's will in the wilderness, we will grow spiritually and become conformed to the image of Jesus Christ.

Fortunately, God never intended for the wilderness to be our final destination. The wilderness is meant to be a place that will bring forth growth and maturity as we pass through it. God's goal, His Promised Land, is the character of Christ within us. We call this spiritual maturity, and when we come to this place in our journey, He will give us a ministry so we can bring others along. More and more in our journey of faith, we will experience fulfillment and joy.

CHAPTER | 10

STRAIGHTENING OUT OUR LIVES

> The voice of him that crieth in the wilderness, Prepare ye the way of the Lord, make straight in the desert a highway for our God. Every valley shall be exalted, and every mountain and hill shall be made low: and the crooked shall be made straight, and the rough places plain.
> —Isaiah 40:3–4 KJV

I remember seeing the Judean wilderness on our first visit to Israel. Our tour guide took my wife and me to the top of a peak where we could look out at the rocky hills, which stood in sharp contrast to the beautiful blue sky and the green groves of date palms in a distant kibbutz. The only roads on which we traveled were man-made. It was difficult to imagine how people in ancient days got from place to place in this difficult climate and rough terrain. It is in this context we can imagine the prophet crying out, "Make straight in the desert a highway for our God."

Hebrews 12:13 says, "and make straight paths for your feet, so that what is lame may not be dislocated, but rather be healed." This text is referring to our walk. How we live our lives matters to God. This Scripture says we will be healed as we walk on straight paths.

How do we make straight paths for our feet? If a bone in our foot is dislocated, a rocky and uneven path would further damage that foot, but a straight path would allow it to heal. In Hebrew, the word for *iniquity* means "bent, twisted or distorted." In the same way, we often use the word *crook* to describe a thief, or *twisted* to describe a pervert.

What God desires most is to heal our character. Our character is formed throughout our life as we make good or bad choices. Good habits are the foundation of good character and bad habits are the foundation of bad character. When we come to Christ, God starts to change the areas of our lives that were formed out of sinful habits.

We must identify and "straighten out" the areas in our lives that are out of line with God's Word. First, we must surrender our lives to God and walk in obedience to His will. I know someone who had a real struggle with alcohol. When he shared his struggle with a friend, the friend asked him when his temptation was greatest. He told him it was when he was on the way home from work and would pass a bar. He would see his friends there and would drop in to say, "Hi." Once inside, he would order an alcoholic drink, and then another—and eventually get drunk. His friend advised him to take a different route home and see what happened. His choice made all the difference in the world. He avoided the temptation until eventually his addiction to alcohol was broken.

This is just one example of how bad habits can be broken by replacing them with good habits. This is one way to make a straight path for your feet. Paul talks about "having your feet shod with the preparation of the Gospel of peace" (Ephesians 6:15). Note that the text refers to the word *preparation of the Gospel of peace* not just the

Gospel of peace. Our walk and our choices prepare the way for the Gospel to be heard.

Our feet represent our walk, which ultimately represents our character, for it is our character that prepares the way before us. If your life matches your message, people are more likely to listen to you when you share the Gospel.

This is why *we* must make the way straight for our God, so that others can find the pathway *to* God. We are preparing a highway where others will walk. It is the pathway to God and is made straight, made clear, when the character of God is reflected in our lives.

The prophet goes on to describe the process of making a straight highway for our God. *Every valley will be exalted.* The valleys in life often speak of disappointment, brokenness and shame. In these times God comes to us in the spirit of encouragement. We are all broken to one degree or another and we all need encouragement. It is the broken places of our lives where God most often begins to work in us. Hosea makes a reference to this:

> Therefore, behold, I will allure her,
> Will bring her into the wilderness,
> And speak comfort to her.
> I will give her vineyards from there,
> And the Valley of Achor as a door of hope.
> —Hosea 2:14–15a

The word *Achor* means "trouble or disturbance." *The Valley of Achor* refers to Israel's past where they were defeated because of the sin of Achan, who stole things given to God (Joshua 7:1–3). The army was defeated because of Achan's sin. It was in this place of defeat that the prophet spoke comfort to God's people. God doesn't reject us because of our failure; He wants us to draw closer to Himself *through* the failure. God wants us to turn to Him when we fail. This is the true meaning of repentance—*turning to God.*

Sin has consequences that can be challenging, but in the place of failure and brokenness, God wants to open a door of hope. God is not condemning us, but welcoming us. This is what it means to "lift up the valleys." As God encourages us in our failures, pouring out His grace, we are able to encourage and comfort others (2 Corinthians 1:4).

The reason that hope is a doorway is because the hard place is temporary, and the place we are going is better. A doorway beckons us to a place of hope, a transition out of a difficult place—but it is not our final destination.

I have a friend who was not open to the Gospel but he was open to me. I had shared my testimony with him and he thought that was good for me but not for him. I hadn't seen him for some time when I received a call from another friend who told me he thought our mutual friend was ready to take an Alpha Course and suggested that I call him since we were running Alpha in our home.

When I called him he was quite surprised at the timing of my call. In fact, he told me that he was amazed because he had a dream two nights earlier about my father and had awakened with a start. In the dream my father was at the end of a long dark tunnel beside a doorway. He was wearing an old, worn winter coat. He was staring at my friend intently with his piercing blue eyes. Without any words being spoken, my friend understood that he was to enter through the doorway. He went through the door into a blue room. At this point, my father vanished, leaving him alone. He sat down on a chair in the blue room, and then he woke up.

The dream seemed so real to him—and he doesn't normally remember his dreams. He asked me if I knew what the dream meant. I told him that I thought I understood the dream. My father had had a difficult life, which was represented by the old winter coat. The long tunnel was the struggle that my friend was going through (although at the time, I didn't know what he was going through). My father came to faith in Christ before he died and he was showing the pathway to my friend. The door represented the door of hope as mentioned in Hosea 2:14–15. The new room represented the place that God had for him. Blue is the color of the sky, which speaks of faith. The chair represented God's rest that we enter by faith (Hebrews 4:10). I invited him to attend our Alpha Course and he did. Eventually he accepted Christ.

God lifted him up, while he was walking through a difficult valley. It was that "lifting up" that brought him to Christ. It is amazing how people respond to the grace of God. As Paul reflects, it is the goodness of God that brings us to repentance (Romans 2:4). Jesus was compassionate and gentle to the broken, the down and out, the prostitutes and tax collectors—but He was harsh with those who thought they had it all together—the Pharisees.

CHAPTER 11

PREPARING OUR MINDS

Several years ago our church bulletin included this gem: "The definition of failure is a success story without God." I like that. As long as people have outward success and don't feel a need for God, they may never find Him. That is a great tragedy, and I thank God for my personal failures and struggles that led me to Him.

In the Bible, those who knew they were sinful received compassion, but the self-righteous were reprimanded severely. The Pharisees were self-righteous and judgmental, and Jesus condemned their proud and arrogant attitudes outright.

Sometimes God has to humble us to get our attention. I have heard of more people coming to Christ out of their need than for any other reason. In the process of showing us our need, God humbles us. His motives are not destructive but redemptive. Psalm 119:67 says, "Before I was afflicted I went astray, but now I keep Your word."

In Isaiah 40, it is the mountains and hills that must be made low. In our lives, any pride, any obstacle that we must overcome by faith, must be made low. Paul spoke about casting down every high thing that exalts itself against the knowledge of God.

> For though we walk in the flesh, we do not war according to the flesh. For the weapons of our warfare are not carnal but mighty in God for pulling down strongholds, casting down arguments and every high thing that exalts itself against the knowledge of God, bringing every thought into captivity to the obedience of Christ, and being ready to punish all disobedience when your obedience is fulfilled. —2 Corinthians 10:3–6

Paul is telling us to identify and reject anything that does not line up with God's Word. Let me give you an example. If you believe that you are worthless and unlovable it will affect the way you behave. And it is not true. God's Word says you are precious, beloved.

Our behavior is determined by what we believe. If we believe wrong ideas, we will behave badly. Millions of Jews were put to death because Hitler persuaded the German people that the Jews were dangerous and needed to be exterminated. The fruit of that lie was bitter—the death of millions of Jews and Gentiles.

Our thinking determines who we become. If we set our minds on negative things, we become negative. If we set our minds on the offenses brought against us, we will become bitter. If we set our minds on money, we become greedy. If we set our minds on Jesus Christ, we become conformed into His image (2 Corinthians 3:18). What we believe controls our behavior. The things we think about and value define our behavior. This is why Paul exhorts us to set our mind on the things above (Colossians 3:1–3).

Romans 8:6 says, "For to be carnally minded is death, but to be spiritually minded is life and peace." If you set your mind on the flesh it will kill you spiritually. We must ask God to replace these negative thoughts with spiritually uplifting thoughts.

We need also to cast down thoughts that cause unbelief or obscure our vision of God. This is no small feat. Our thought patterns may have given us problems for years. They may be what the Bible refers to as strongholds. Just as a fortress holds captives, these strongholds hold us captive to sin. But there is good news! Jesus came to set the captives free! The Word of God assures us that the weapons we possess *guarantee* our success on one condition—full obedience to God (2 Corinthians 10:6).

It is important to understand that it is not our feelings that guarantee success; they will almost always guarantee failure. Rather, it is our obedience to the Word of God, sometimes in spite of our feelings, that guarantees success. As we submit to God and His Word, we cast down false ideas and strongholds that have held us captive and in Him we secure victory.

Our feelings indicate what we believe. If we are fearful or anxious, at some level we believe something that makes us feel that way. We may not be aware of it, but our feelings expose what is there. Rather than giving into negative feelings, and letting them run your life, take them to God. Ask yourself, "What do I believe that makes me feel this way? And is it true?" Let God's Word speak life into your places of pain so you can cast down false ideas and strongholds that have held you captive. In that way we can know truth in our inward parts and move into wholeness. We want what we feel in our heart to be in agreement with what we know in our head, so we can live a victorious life.

One of the strongholds that I had to overcome was thinking that I couldn't be Jewish and believe in Jesus. If you ask a typical Jew, he will tell you that Jews don't believe in Jesus. When I came to faith in Jesus Christ, to my astonishment and delight I found that being Jewish was completely compatible with believing in Jesus. It wasn't compatible with traditional Judaism, but it was compatible with being Jewish. Jesus was a Jew and the true Messiah of Israel. So even though most Jews don't believe in Jesus, their unbelief doesn't change His identity—and it didn't change mine, either.

Years ago a Jewish person came to my house to find out why we had converted to Christianity. In her mind we were no longer Jewish. We had just come back from a holiday in Israel. I was sharing about our trip, when she stopped me and said, "Harvey you are so Jewish, tell me, what do you believe?" I told her my story and she said that it was the first time she had heard that a person could believe in Jesus and still be Jewish. Strongholds of unbelief can hold a person utterly captive.

Another stronghold that prevents people from coming to faith is the feeling of unworthiness. They believe they are so bad that God cannot forgive them. This is unbiblical and unbalanced. People who have great remorse over their failures and inadequacies can come to Jesus, find forgiveness, and new life—but often their unbelief stops them. They need to find out what the Bible says about God's unconditional love and His offer of eternal life (John 3:16).

There are so many strongholds—more than can be mentioned here. We can take offence at a Christian's behavior, which can hinder our coming to faith. We can be blinded by scientific theories such as evolution. Thank God there are believers who are scientists and who are able to explain some of the apparent discrepancies between science and faith. My brother Howard, an engineer, gives a slide presentation entitled, "Noah's Ark and the Flood: Is it Scientifically Possible?" He presents a credible scientific basis for believing the historic evidence for a worldwide flood. This presentation has helped believers and seekers alike.

The foundation for all unbelief is *pride* which is defined as "self in control." Since the Garden of Eden, people have rebelled against God and tried to take charge of their own lives (Genesis 3). Faith in Christ restores humankind to God's order for living. The way to combat unbelief is by faith and the way to get faith is by hearing God's Word. Romans 10:17 says, "So then faith comes by hearing, and hearing by the word of God."

You should never hesitate to ask hard questions. There are answers. If you have questions, take the opportunity to investigate. You will discover that there are many wonderful resources which can put your doubts to rest.

For example, one organization called Reasons to Believe presents scientific evidence for God, working with believers and seekers to show them how science and faith can come together. Truth can stand the most vigorous of investigations. Accept the challenge!

CHAPTER 12

LETTING GOD REFINE US

> Every valley shall be raised up,
> every mountain and hill made low;
> the rough ground shall become level,
> and the rugged places a plain.
> —Isaiah 40:4 NIV

Isn't it funny that sandpaper makes things smooth? I was refinishing some outdoor wooden chairs the other day. The wood had become weathered and bleached from the sun and wind, so I tried to blast them with a pressure washer to peel off the old layers of stain, but this only made the wood splinter. They needed a good sanding.

I called my neighbor who has all the neat little gadgets and tools, and asked him if he had a little palm sander. He immediately brought one over and within an hour I had sanded the wood even and smooth. I coated the wood with new stain, which was absorbed evenly because the wood was prepared to receive the stain. God uses "sandpaper" circumstances and the people in our lives to smooth out our rough edges.

Isaiah 40:4 says, "The crooked places shall be made straight, And the rough places smooth." The word used here for *crooked places* is "akov" the same root word used for the name, *Jacob*. Jacob got his name because he grabbed his twin brother, Esau's, heel at birth. *Jacob* means "he grasps the heel" or is a "supplanter," which in Hebrew means "he deceives." Jacob was crooked before God straightened him out. The name was a prophetic picture of the day when *Jacob* would "supplant" Esau.

Names are highly significant in the Bible, often describing either the character of the person or the work that God was going to accomplish through him. Jacob obtained the blessing and the birthright through cunning and manipulation (Genesis 27:36).

Although Jacob was crafty at taking care of himself, through a series of divine circumstances God brought him to a place where he could no longer depend on his own abilities. In Genesis 32, Jacob was returning to his homeland with his family after having been away for many years. He would soon meet the brother he had defrauded of the special blessing that was reserved for the firstborn. Jacob knew he had wronged Esau, and back when the whole incident occurred, Esau had vowed to kill Jacob (Genesis 27:41). Now Jacob was heading home and would have to face his brother. After sending his family on ahead, Jacob spent the night alone. On that dark lonely night, Jacob wrestled with the Angel of Lord, believed by some Biblical scholars to be the pre-incarnate Christ.

Before dawn, the Angel touched the hollow of Jacob's thigh and caused him to be crippled, but Jacob still would not let go. The Angel told Jacob to release him because dawn was breaking, but Jacob refused until the Angel blessed him. The Angel of the Lord then changed Jacob's name to Israel and blessed him. From that point onward Jacob walked with a limp. Jacob named the place *Peniel* meaning, "I saw the face of God and lived."

This story depicts the personal transformation of Jacob. The occasion marked his "dark night of the soul." He was alone, bereft of all human resources and dreading the possibility of meeting his brother Esau, who might have revenge on his mind. In this dark place, Jacob wrestled with God until he obtained a breakthrough. The struggle left him with a limp. He could no longer depend on his own strength, but had to depend on God. His limp was a new walk in life. His new name symbolized the new character within him: he was no longer the old crooked Jacob, he was the new *Israel*—"Prince with God." By the grace of God, Jacob became an overcomer.

God often does the same thing in our lives. He gets us alone so that He can do a deep spiritual work in us. It can be a lonely and dark place. God may hurt us, but He will never harm us. His wounds are meant to bring life, cleansing and healing. This preparatory work allows Him to make the "crooked places" straight. Jacob had a destiny to fulfill, something he couldn't do as the old Jacob, only as the new Israel. Like Jacob, each of us also has a destiny to fulfill.

God accepts us as we are, but fortunately He doesn't leave us that way. God's unconditional love means that He will continue to love us in spite of our rebellion and sin and will continue to work out His plan for our lives. His plan is to form within us the character of Christ (Galatians 4:19), and He will do it by disciplining us in love, just as good parents discipline their children because they want to form good moral character within them.

CHAPTER 13

CHARACTER VERSUS CHARISMA? GOD'S PRIORITY

King Saul learned the hard way. God had told him to utterly destroy the Amalekites and not take any spoil from among their goods. In accordance with God's plan, King Saul attacked the Amalekites and was victorious over them. But contrary to God's instructions, Saul let Agag, king of the Amalekites live, and also kept the best of the sheep to sacrifice to God. It is here that we pick up the narrative of the story.

> "Why then did you not obey the voice of the LORD? Why did you swoop down on the spoil, and do evil in the sight of the LORD?"
>
> And Saul said to Samuel, "But I have obeyed the voice of the LORD, and gone on the mission on which the LORD sent me, and brought back Agag king of Amalek; I have utterly destroyed the Amalekites. But the people took of the plunder, sheep and oxen, the best of the things which should have been utterly destroyed, to sacrifice to the LORD your God in Gilgal."
>
> So Samuel said:
> Has the LORD as great delight in burnt offerings and sacrifices,

As in obeying the voice of the LORD?
Behold, to obey is better than sacrifice,
And to heed than the fat of rams.
For rebellion is as the sin of witchcraft,
And stubbornness is as iniquity and idolatry.
Because you have rejected the word of the LORD,
He also has rejected you from being king."
—1 Samuel 15:19–23

Did you notice how defensive Saul was? "I did obey," he protested. Look at the results—I have taken captive Agag king of the Amalekites and kept the best of the sheep and goats to sacrifice to the Lord your God.

The reality was that Saul was obedient on *his* terms but not on *God's* terms. As far as Saul was concerned he was completely successful. He had won the battle, destroyed the people of Amalek, taken their king captive, and kept the best sheep and oxen for a sacrifice. But in God's eyes, Saul had failed because he did what made sense to him instead of obeying all that God told him to do.

God says, "To obey is better than sacrifice, and to heed than the fat of rams." Quite frankly, Saul lost his kingdom because he valued self-will more than obedience, and made the grave mistake of thinking that he was successful because of his apparent good results.

Saul's triumph was very short lived, and eventually he became a miserable, insecure, jealous man who lost his family, his kingdom and his life—all as a result of his disobedience! It is a warning that we should all heed. Saul was concerned about outward success but had little regard for inward sanctification. God is more concerned about our inward life than about our natural abilities and credentials—more concerned with *who* we are than *what we do.* God values *being* over *doing.*

When God chose David, the Scriptures tell us that He first rejected David's older brothers. Look at what Samuel thought when he first saw David's older brothers:

> So it was, when they came, that he looked at Eliab and said, "Surely the LORD's anointed is before Him!" But the LORD said to Samuel, "Do not look at his appearance or at his physical stature, because I have refused him. For the LORD does not see as man sees; for man looks at the outward appearance, but the LORD looks at the heart."
>
> —1 Samuel 16:6–7

Notice what the Scriptures say: The Lord does not see as a man sees, for man looks at the *outward appearance* but the Lord looks at the *heart*. People value good looks, intelligence, and material success—to name but a few. But the God who provides these things is not impressed. God's gaze pierces through to the soul.

David loved God with his whole heart. When no one else was looking, God was watching David as he tended sheep and He saw his heart. During those times of solitude, David was being prepared for greatness, as he built a strong relationship with God. David had no idea that God was preparing him to shepherd His people Israel. David demonstrated his love and trust for God over and over again. David trusted God in the most desperate circumstances, not even seeking revenge against his enemies. And even when David sinned, his repentance was sincere and heartfelt.

These godly qualities make David a role model for us. His life proves that God does not choose us because of our looks, our abilities, or our intelligence, although He can certainly use those things.

He chooses us because of His grace and love for us, and as we respond to God's love, He wants to change us on the inside to become conformed to the image of His Son Jesus Christ (Romans 8:29).

As we respond to the Holy Spirit, our character becomes more like Jesus. It is out of this refined character that we are able to minister the Gospel to others. One contemporary example is Dale Lang, whose son Jason was murdered by a fourteen-year-old student at W.R. Myers High School in Taber, Alberta on April 28, 1999. Despite the overwhelming loss and grief he felt as a father, Dale chose to forgive the confused young man who killed his son.

His godly response to heartbreaking tragedy has provided opportunity for Dale to speak all across Canada about the need for forgiveness and about the grace of the Lord Jesus Christ. Dale commented, "as someone who had been a follower of Jesus Christ for twenty-two years, forgiveness was the only response that I could give. I didn't think about it, my wife and I didn't sit down and talk about it; it was a response out of our faith. We did it because it was the way we understood Who Jesus is. And we did that and it had a significant impact on people in the country. I cannot explain except to say that people just are not used to forgiveness."[2]

This is just one example of how character has won out over charisma to win the hearts of those who need Jesus Christ. I don't know much about Dale Lang. I don't know if he likes golf. I don't know if he is brilliant. I don't know if he is athletic. But I do know that Dale Lang lost his son in a terrible tragedy that would have ruined the lives of most people—and he *chose* to forgive because he is a Christian. The other things don't matter. This single act of grace has demonstrated the character of Christ in his life more than everything else combined.

We don't need a great tragedy to be witnesses for the Gospel, but we do need to allow our lives to be used in a way that brings glory to God. Each of us has the potential to let Christ's light shine to light the way for others.

We may feel we are inadequate and immature, and question whether we can be a light to others. However, the path we are on is more important than our level of maturity. Some people who have been believers for many years have stopped growing spiritually and consequently have ceased to be effective witnesses. As we continue to walk in the light we have, God uses us where we are. We cannot take someone farther than we have come, but we can share with them what we know.

CHAPTER 14

BEING FILLED WITH THE SPIRIT

Whatever method you use to share the Gospel, the only effective witness is one empowered by the Spirit of God. If the method doesn't leave room for the work of the Holy Spirit, this does not mean people will not come to Christ, but our witness will not be as effective. Paul recognized that some people proclaimed Christ for the wrong motives and he rejoiced because God can use even this (Philippians 1:18):

> But you shall receive power when the Holy Spirit has come upon you; and you shall be witnesses to Me in Jerusalem, and in all Judea and Samaria, and to the end of the earth.
>
> —Acts 1:8

Did you notice the order? First, you receive power and then you witness for Christ. If you have learned anything from this book, I hope it will be that without the power of God, you yourself can do nothing! God hasn't asked you to do something on your own. This is terrific news because God *can* do it through you (Philippians 4:13)! Do you remember the mountains and hills mentioned in the last section? One of the mountains to overcome is fear. Being filled with God's Spirit will give you power over the fear of sharing the Good News.

> "And when they had prayed, the place where they were assembled together was shaken; and **they were all filled with the Holy Spirit, and they spoke the word of God with boldness."**
> —Acts 4:31

Notice the order again. They were "filled with the Holy Spirit" and "spoke the Word of God with boldness." We cannot minister fully unless the Holy Spirit is operating in our lives. How did the followers of Jesus get that power? Scripture says "when they prayed they were filled." We need to pray to be filled with the Spirit so we can be bold witnesses for Christ. Unless we ask to be filled with the Spirit, we will lack something.

Indeed, Paul commanded the believers in Ephesus to be filled with the Spirit. Ephesians 5:18 says, "And do not be drunk with wine, in which is dissipation; **but be filled with the Spirit**." This was a command given to believers. Unless we are filled with the Spirit, we will not be effective in our witness for Christ. Even Paul recognized the ineffectiveness of his own efforts when he asked the Christians at Ephesus to pray that he might have boldness.

> . . . praying always with all prayer and supplication in the Spirit, being watchful to this end with all perseverance and supplication for all the saints—and for me, that utterance may be given to me, that I may open my mouth boldly to make known the mystery of the Gospel, for which I am an ambassador in chains; that in it I may speak boldly, as I ought to speak.
> —Ephesians 6:18–20

Once when I was sharing my testimony at a young adult's Bible study, a woman came up to me and said, "I have taught Sunday school for years, but I don't have what you have. How can I be filled with the Spirit?" This took me by surprise because I hadn't spoken about being filled with the Spirit, yet she felt compelled to ask for it. She certainly asked the right question!

When we are filled with the Spirit, not only will we speak boldly, but others will see a difference and want what we have.

How to Be Filled with the Holy Spirit

The Bible often speaks about being filled with the Spirit. This subject alone could fill a whole book. I am going to highlight only a few points on being filled with the Holy Spirit.

The first condition to be filled with the Holy Spirit is faith. Galatians 3:2 says, "This only I want to learn from you: Did you **receive** the Spirit by the works of the law, or by the hearing of **faith?**" Later, in the same chapter Paul again writes, "that the blessing of Abraham might come upon the Gentiles in Christ Jesus, that we might **receive** the promise of the Spirit through **faith**" (Galatians 3:14).

Did you notice that I emphasized the words *receive* and *faith*? We don't earn the filling of the Spirit, we receive it as a gift. Some people don't receive the infilling of the Holy Spirit because they don't feel worthy and therefore cannot receive it. If we look to our feelings then we probably won't receive. We don't walk by feelings but by faith and that faith is based on the Word of God. I have often told people to stand in faith on God's Word and believe God for this baptism of the Holy Spirit. The condition for receiving the infilling of the Holy Spirit is that it be received through faith.

Next, we receive the Holy Spirit by asking. Luke 11:13 says, "If you then, being evil, know how to give good gifts to your children, how much more will your heavenly Father **give the Holy Spirit to those who ask Him!"**

Jesus says we must *ask for the Holy Spirit.* We can ask God for the Holy Spirit in prayer—simple conversation with God. We don't come to God because we are worthy, but because we are His children. We can ask Him for anything. Think how happy He will be to give us the infilling of His Holy Spirit! In the book of Acts, the Apostles were commanded to wait in Jerusalem for the gift of the Holy Spirit (Acts 1:4–8). While they prayed and waited, they were filled with the Holy Spirit on the day of Pentecost.

When they were filled with the Holy Spirit, they spoke in tongues as the Spirit enabled them (Acts 2:4). We see over and over again that when people are filled with the Spirit they speak in tongues (Acts 10:44–48; 19:1–6). Speaking in tongues is not the infilling of the Holy Spirit but it is the *initial evidence* of having received this gift. Speaking in tongues is primarily a prayer tool (1 Corinthians 14:2) that builds us up spiritually—especially for witnessing.

When the believers were filled with the Holy Spirit and spoke in other tongues, pilgrims from foreign lands heard them speaking in their own language glorifying God! (Acts 2:5–11). That day over 3000 people gave their lives to the Lord. This is just one example of how being filled with the Spirit and speaking in tongues can draw people to Jesus.

Speaking in another language by the power of the Holy Spirit seems an outrageous idea to most people who are unfamiliar with its origins. That is because it is a supernatural act. Yet it is one that clearly was made available to all believers after Jesus left the earth. He had promised His followers that when He was gone, the Father would send the Holy Spirit to those who believed in His name. And it is by the power of the Holy Spirit that this unusual manifestation occurs.

Speaking in tongues is mostly used in private prayer, to prepare us for the work of God. One person I know prays in tongues every morning for fifteen minutes in addition to praying with her own understanding. This person felt that it transformed her ministry in reaching the lost.

Many of God's children experience dramatic changes in their ministry when they receive the infilling of the Holy Spirit. I have seen this in my personal experience as well as in the Scriptures.

If you are not sure how to pray to receive the infilling of the Holy Spirit then perhaps this prayer will help you:

> Dear Lord, I am Your child because of what Jesus Christ did on the cross for me. Thank You that He died for my sins and rose again. I believe that You want me to be filled with Your Holy Spirit. I surrender my life to You completely and ask you to forgive all my sins so that I can be used by You. Please take all of my life and fill me with Your Holy Spirit now. I ask this in Jesus' name. Amen.

If you have prayed that prayer by faith, then you are filled with the Holy Spirit. You may have felt a physical touch of the Holy Spirit such as tingling, heat or some other physical sensation. You may not have felt anything. It is not the feeling that is important, it is the faith. The gift of speaking in tongues is now available to you.

Try to speak forth words by faith, trusting in the Holy Spirit to pray through you. If nothing happens don't be troubled but rest in the faithfulness of God. He will answer your prayer. Sometimes it helps to have someone who has already experienced the infilling of the Holy Spirit pray with you by faith. Their faith will encourage you to receive this gift.

Some are confused by tongues. They think they will lose control of their mouth. They worry that they will babble uncontrollably, but you can start or stop speaking in tongues at any time. You control that part. You won't speak in tongues against your will. You have to let air out to speak. What God controls is what words form as the sound comes out. The words may sound strange to you at first, but they are your spirit crying out to God in a perfect language that He has given you.

The whole point of receiving power from God is to be a bold witness for Christ. The gifts of the Holy Spirit are not limited to speaking in tongues. God has provided a whole range of spiritual gifts for our benefit and His glory (1 Corinthians 12:1–12). Paul gives instructions on the proper use of the gifts of the Holy Spirit in 1 Corinthians, Chapter 14.

I am convinced that without the infilling of the Holy Spirit and walking in the Spirit as we trust in Christ daily, we will be ineffective. The prophet Isaiah exhorts us to "cry out!" We cry out by the power of God within us. It is His power and His life that changes us and touches the world.

CHAPTER 15

HINDRANCES TO RECEIVING THE BAPTISM OF THE HOLY SPIRIT

If you pray and nothing seems to happen, take it to the Lord. I have a friend who prayed to be filled with the Holy Spirit and receive the gift of tongues, but nothing seemed to happen. He asked the Lord and the Lord told him that he needed to go to his father and ask his father to forgive him. He obeyed. That evening, in the quiet of his home, he found he was able to speak in tongues.

Some people struggle to enter into the baptism of the Holy Spirit. When nothing seems to happen, some feel unworthy, but none of us is worthy, so being worthy can never be a condition for being filled with the Holy Spirit. We receive the baptism of the Holy Spirit by faith.

There are three hindrances to faith. The first one is unbelief. This may seem obvious because unbelief is the opposite of faith and we must have faith to be filled with the Spirit. But if you don't believe in the experience, it will be hard to have the faith that God is going to fill you. I ask people who don't believe to read what the

Bible says about being filled, so they can see what the Bible says and believe.

Fear is a second reason people struggle with the concept of the infilling of the Holy Spirit. Fear is another form of unbelief. Some people are afraid that nothing will happen, and that quenches their faith. Others are afraid of what might happen. They are afraid of losing control or looking foolish or any number of other fears. The supernatural can be frightening because we feel we are letting go of control. Some people are afraid that it is demonic instead of godly. All of these notions can be hindrances to entering into the baptism of the Holy Spirit.

A third obstacle is unconfessed sin. When someone sins willfully and does not confess that sin, it creates a block in the person's relationship with God. I am not trying to say that we must be perfect, but deliberate, willful, unconfessed sin erects a wall between God and us. One of the most willful sins is unforgiveness toward those who have hurt us. Unforgiveness stops the flow of God's grace in our lives and hinders us from receiving the baptism of the Holy Spirit.

If you feel blocked, ask God for help and insight. If something comes to mind, confess it before God and confidently ask Him to fill you with His Holy Spirit.

My brother, Howard, waited many years to be baptized in the Holy Spirit even though as a new Christian he earnestly sought the experience. Numerous times he went forward for prayer during church services seeking the baptism.

One time, he even fasted and prayed all night to be baptized with the Spirit. For a number of years, not only did he not receive it, but when others were feeling the tangible presence of God, he felt nothing.

Over time he became more and more discouraged until he stopped seeking the baptism of the Holy Spirit. At this point the baptism of the Holy Spirit became a painful topic. He felt it was unattainable for him.

He continued to attend a Pentecostal church and was actively involved in its youth ministry, but he had resigned himself to the fact that he might never receive the baptism of the Holy Spirit. When altar calls were given for those who wanted to receive this baptism, he no longer went forward since it always ended in frustration.

After Howard had been a Christian for seventeen years, God began to birth a new hunger within him to receive the baptism of the Holy Spirit. For a number of months the desire grew and began to push back the earlier years of discouragement.

One day a prophetic brother who was visiting had a "word of knowledge" for him. It was a gentle word of encouragement that reassured Howard of God's faithfulness. The message to Howard was that even during times of discouragement, God would be faithful.

At the time Howard did not know what this "word" referred to, but two weeks later a missionary came to visit the church. While the missionary was there the church held nightly prayer meetings. One night, during one of the prayer meetings, the missionary encouraged people to seek the baptism of the Holy Spirit and shared a prophetic word that "the singer will sing."

This last reference was to someone who was going to be filled with the Spirit. This prophetic word stirred expectation and hope in Howard. Then the Pastor asked if anyone wanted to be baptized in the Holy Spirit. Howard struggled. Part of him wanted to experience more of God but the other part feared more failure. He did not want to be humiliated in front of everyone, when they saw, once again, no evidence of infilling. But the desire was so great within him that he stepped forward, fell on his knees and said, "I want to be baptized in the Holy Spirit."

Even though there were several people present who had not been baptized in the Holy Spirit, Howard was the only one that came forward. As everyone began to pray with raised voices, Howard battled self-consciousness. *How can I receive it?* he wondered. *What will others think if I do not?* Then Howard remembered the advice that his mother-in-law had given him a few days before: "Keep your thoughts on Christ and just worship Him. Do not let yourself be self-conscious."

As he prayed, focusing on the Lord Jesus, he experienced a very tangible manifestation of the Holy Spirit. It was as if a glass dome filled with cool air slipped over him starting at his head and moving down to his waist. As it did, the sounds of others praying stilled, as if they had moved far away. He began to shake uncontrollably. He tried to receive the baptism of the Holy Spirit. After several minutes, this intense experience lifted. He was very encouraged.

Later that evening, Howard experienced the same sense of cool air slipping over him, but as before, it ended without him speaking in tongues.

He went home that night encouraged and determined, thinking, *Tomorrow night I will receive the baptism of the Holy Spirit!* The next day he fasted in preparation for the evening meeting. That night, Howard had a powerful experience of the presence of God, but failed to receive fully. During one experience of the presence, he even silently said to God the words that Jacob spoke when he wrestled with God, "I will not let You go until You bless me." But all these attempts ended without success.

Howard felt weary physically and emotionally. He went home that night thinking he may be one of those who will never receive this gift. Waves of condemnation flowed over him. He felt himself a failure. He did not even go to bed, but threw himself on the couch. About 2 A.M. he woke up, filled with an overwhelming sense of despair and self-pity. He was on the verge of falling into the same depression and despair that had entrapped him many years before when he had first sought the baptism of the Holy Spirit.

In a step of faith, he fell on his knees and began to worship God. He said, "Even if I do not receive the baptism of the Holy Spirit, I will praise You." With a heavy heart he began to praise God. As he did, the words of prophesy that were given to him earlier came to him: "During a time of discouragement, take courage. God will be faithful to you." This was that time. He was certain. Faith in God's faithfulness suddenly began to grow in his heart, as he thought on that prophetic word and continued to praise the Lord.

As he praised, a new resolve to seek the baptism of the Holy Spirit came to him. He knew there would be a prayer meeting that night and he decided to phone the pastor in the morning and ask him to pray with him before the meeting. Peace came over Howard and he went back to sleep.

That afternoon, Howard met with the pastor and a few others, and they too began to pray. As they prayed, Howard continued to struggle. He was full of doubt, then someone spoke a simple prophetic word, "Do not be afraid!" As soon as he heard those words, the full impact came to him. "God is faithful to you. You do not need to be afraid, because He is for you and not against you and He will be faithful to baptize you in the Holy Spirit."

As he continued to pray, he relaxed. He again felt a manifestation of the Spirit, but this time it was a little different than before. He felt something glittering over his head, like a small cloud. After the prayer, the pastor said that while they had been praying he saw the glory of God hovering just above Howard's head. This greatly encouraged Howard. God was on the move! Howard's heart filled with faith.

By now it was time for the evening prayer meeting to begin. As they joined the larger group and began to pray, Howard was more relaxed but still exerting effort to keep his mind focused on Christ. As he continued to praise the Lord, all of a sudden he heard some syllables or babbling come out of his mouth "Ba, ba, ba." It had begun without him being aware of it. As soon as he noticed it he thought, *Am I making this up?* Then he thought, *Stop trying to figure it out and focus on Jesus.* As he placed his thoughts on Christ without trying to stop what was coming out of his mouth, all of a sudden he had a vision. He saw clouds above him. Then he saw them part and a bright light appeared. It was as if he no longer had to try to focus his thoughts on the Lord because he was drawn to the Lord.

Howard said it felt like two magnets, drawn together. At first it was as if two magnets of the same polarity were being forced together. Now one magnet had flipped and they were instantly pulled together. He no longer had to force himself to stay focused on God. He was drawn to God.

He felt himself being caught up toward the light. In the middle of this overwhelming experience, he heard someone singing in trill. *It was he! The singer had begun to sing!* From that moment forward, Howard experienced a new freedom in prayer and a heart full of joy.

CHAPTER 16

HOW POWER AND GLORY ATTRACT PEOPLE TO JESUS

> The glory of the LORD shall be revealed,
> And all flesh shall see it together;
> For the mouth of the LORD has spoken.
> —Isaiah 40:5

This Scripture passage shows us that three things will happen: First, the glory of the Lord shall be revealed. The word *reveal* comes from the word "revelation." God will reveal Jesus Christ through you. It is not what you say that makes you a credible witness; it is who God is and what He says that makes you credible. The word, which has been translated *glory*, is the same word used for "honor." Paul speaks of "Christ in you, the hope of glory" (Colossians 1:27). Christ dwells within us by His Spirit, and it is this reality that God demonstrates to the world around us.

The second thing we need to know is that "all flesh shall see it together." God's glory in earthen vessels will be obvious to everyone. However, some people will be attracted to the glory of the Lord in our lives; and others will be repelled. Paul said that to some we are the fragrance of life and to others the smell of death (2 Corinthians 2:16).

Either way, when God's glory is shining in our lives, it is undeniable. People might not understand what they see, but they will know that there is something special and unique about our lives.

Paul admits that he did not come with convincing words, but by a demonstration of the Spirit's power. First Corinthians 2:4 says, "And my speech and my preaching were not with persuasive words of human wisdom, but in demonstration of the Spirit and of power." The book of Acts gives us many examples of how the Holy Spirit worked through the Apostles to bring people to Christ.

Here are some demonstrations of the Spirit's power:

> "Now, LORD, look on their threats, and grant to Your servants that with all boldness they may speak Your word, by stretching out Your hand to heal, and that signs and wonders may be done through the name of Your holy servant Jesus."
>
> And when they had prayed, the place where they were assembled together was shaken; and they were all filled with the Holy Spirit, and they spoke the word of God with boldness.
>
> —Acts 4:29-31

> There he found a certain man named Aeneas, who had been bedridden eight years and was paralyzed. And Peter said to him, "Aeneas, Jesus the Christ heals you. Arise and make your bed." Then he arose immediately. So all who dwelt at Lydda and Sharon saw him and turned to the LORD.
>
> —Acts 9:33-35

What demonstrations? The place shook. They were filled with the Holy Spirit and spoke the Word of God with boldness. The lame walked. The manifestations may be varied, but they all point to Christ.

The third thing that will happen is that the Lord will speak to His people. The glory of the Lord is connected with the proclamation of the Word of God.

> So shall My word be that goes forth from My mouth;
> It shall not return to Me void,
> But it shall accomplish what I please,
> And it shall prosper in the thing for which I sent it.
> —Isaiah 55:11

Amos said that people are dying to hear the Word of God.

> "Behold, the days are coming," says the LORD GOD,
> "That I will send a famine on the land,
> Not a famine of bread,
> Nor a thirst for water,
> But of hearing the words of the LORD."
> —Amos 8:11

Today it seems many people—even believers—have limited knowledge of the Bible. The expression, "You may be the only Bible some people ever read," is true. All that some people will know will be what they see in our lives. There is a famine of God's Word, but we are living epistles sent from God to touch and influence the lives of others (2 Corinthians 3:1-2). Jesus was the living Word sent from heaven to reach us. In the same way, as Spirit-filled believers in Jesus, we are sent by God to reach a dying world with the message of salvation.

How do you put this into practice? When do you know that God is going to do a miracle or some fantastic thing? This is where "the rubber hits the road." If the power of God is not working in my life then it is just another theory. I would like to share with you just one of many stories of how the power of God has worked in my life in a way that I was able to give glory to God and bring others to Jesus.

There was a time in my life when I believed God worked supernaturally but mostly in other people's lives. It was not that I had not experienced God, but I found it hard to believe that God wanted to use me in an extraordinary way. I don't know why I felt that way but I did. It was a real hindrance in my life to trust God for bigger things.

This story was a turning point for me. Many years ago now, I was managing a business that required staffing seven days per week. One Monday morning, I arrived in my usual manner to pick up the weekend cash deposits and take them to the bank when I noticed that one of the deposits was missing.

I double-checked the safe where the money was kept during the weekend and I couldn't find it. My first reaction to this dilemma was that there must have been some kind of mistake, but as I checked everywhere for the money, there was a sickening feeling in my stomach that one of my weekend staff had stolen the money.

I phoned the police while I was still in a daze and reported the incident. An officer was immediately dispatched and met with me that morning. I recounted to him all the details of my missing cash deposit (which was a few thousand dollars). Someone who had access to the safe had stolen the money. There were over 20 staff members had who worked that weekend who then became suspects.

After hearing my story, the officer told me that in cases like these, the thief would never be caught. There were too many people who could have been suspects and not enough evidence to prove who had done it. The officer gave me an occurrence report so that I could claim my losses for my insurance policy but that was the least of my worries. I felt betrayed by someone who worked for me but I did not even know who it was. This left me shocked and angry.

I also felt stupid. I should have had a better system in place to protect the company's cash. I asked the police officer to interview the staff to see if they could find some clues to the mystery of the stolen money. He asked me to contact them and he would interview them.

That day he interviewed several of the staff who were available. There were no confessions, no proof of who stole the money, and I was no further ahead. I was frustrated.

The next day, I was having lunch with my friend Clyde and I was sharing with him the story and all my frustrations regarding the situation. He listened to me patiently and waited until I was finished with my ranting and raving. He gently asked me if he could pray for me so that God could supernaturally reveal to me who stole the money.

I asked him to pray for me, but I was thinking to myself, "Why would God reveal to me who stole the money when it was partly my fault?" Clyde prayed a simple but bold prayer that God would reveal to me the person who stole the money. After we prayed, I remembered something I had dreamed the previous evening, after the theft had occurred. Somehow Clyde's prayer quickened the dream to my memory.

In the dream, I had seen a specific employee take money out of the safe. This was curious, because this employee had asked me the previous week if he could have his next week's paycheck a few days early as he was leaving the following Wednesday on a trip out of the country and needed the money. Now it was Tuesday of the "next week", and he would be leaving the following day.

I immediately shared the dream with Clyde and then prayed that God would confirm whether the dream was from Him or not. How does God confirm something like this? I know that I was not supposed to help God out. What I mean by this is that I was not going to phone the employee and accuse him of stealing or take any foolish step like that. I was trusting God for the next step.

Later that day, I discovered that this employee had left his shift on the weekend for a few minutes and then returned. He then did not show up for work on the Monday, citing car trouble. This did not actually prove anything but was rather suspicious. This all came to light after my prayer with Clyde.

That night (Tuesday), I had another dream about the same employee. In the dream I was on the phone with the employee and asked him to come in and pick up his pay check. He told me that he couldn't come to get it. I had this little argument with him that he must come in and he kept telling me that he couldn't. The dream then switched and I was in my brother Howard's office. I was behind the desk and he was in front of me. I remember asking him, "Did you take the money?" To which he replied, "Yes I did."

The next day I phoned Clyde and shared the dream with him and he felt that this was God's confirmation. I told Howard about the dream and we prayed together for direction. I proceeded to phone the police and request that they interview the employee in question. The officer asked me to contact the employee first and they would come shortly afterward.

I called him several times until he finally answered the phone. I told him that I had his paycheck to give him. He told me his girlfriend would come and get the check. I told him that I needed him to get it. He started to argue with me, telling me that he was busy and he did not have time to come and get it. I told him that something serious had happened and that I needed to see him. He finally agreed, but only reluctantly. When I hung up the phone, I was surprised how similar this experience was to my dream.

I phoned the police and two officers came to my office. When my employee arrived, I handed him his paycheck and one of the officers took him into Howard's office for an interview. I had told the police officers about the circumstantial evidence against him but did not tell them about my dream.

The first officer came out twenty minutes later and looked me straight in the eyes and said, "You've got the wrong guy, this kid is innocent." He told me that he really put the pressure on him and he was as cool as a cucumber. The officer explained that he is trained to get this kind of information out of people and the employee passed the test with flying colors.

At that moment, I thought that I had made a mistake in believing my dream was from God. I offered a quick but silent prayer to God thanking Him for being in control and trusting Him with the outcome of the situation, whatever was going to happen. I refused to allow confusion to dominate my thinking.

The other police officer asked to speak with the employee alone. He met with him in Howard's office and came out five or ten minutes later and said to me, "You'll get your money but you won't get criminal charges." I asked him to explain and he said that the employee wanted to speak to me alone.

At that point I went into Howard's office where the employee was in front of Howard's desk and I went behind it facing him. He started to cry telling me that the second officer had explained to him that our family was very important to the community and had done many good things. I was perplexed and I asked him, "Did you take the money?" He replied, "Yes I did!" These were the very words and in the very room of the dream. It was from God.

I came out from behind the desk and put my hand on his shoulder and said to him, "I forgive you." I had to terminate him from that position because trust had been broken but I offered him a job in another department that did not handle cash. He declined and he repaid most of the money, some of which had been spent fixing up the car that had broken down!

This experience gave me the confidence to believe God for greater things. I have shared this story with many people who have been amazed at God's power and glory. It has been instrumental in sharing my faith journey and leading others to find Christ themselves. This is just one powerful example from my own life as to how the power and the glory of Christ is revealed in our lives in such a way that others see the hand of God.

This brings us to the last theme entitled "Presentation: One Message, Many Methods."

PART 3

PRESENTATION: *One Message, Many Methods*

The voice said, "Cry out!"
And he said, "What shall I cry?"
"All flesh is grass,
And all its loveliness is like the flower of the field.
The grass withers, the flower fades,
Because the breath of the LORD blows upon it;
Surely the people are grass.
The grass withers, the flower fades,
But the word of our God stands forever."
—Isaiah 40:6–8

Sometimes it seems that we spend so long in processes of *Identification* and *Preparation* that we will never get to the stage of *Presentation.* In the first two themes above, we focused on building relationships with others and building character within ourselves. In this theme, which I call *presentation,* or *proclamation,* I would like to explore methods of sharing the Good News. We will use Isaiah 40:6–8 as the outline for this discussion in which we hope to answer three basic questions: What to share? When to share? How to share?

CHAPTER 17

WHAT TO SHARE

> The voice said, "Cry out!"
> And he said, "What shall I cry?"
> —Isaiah 40:6

The Hebrew verb *cry* is an imperative; it is a command! The word *cry* here can mean "to call, to cry out, to preach, to invite." All of those definitions are helpful because in evangelism we proclaim, we preach, we invite and we call out the Gospel of Jesus Christ. Sharing our faith with others is not an option, it is a command; and it is one of the greatest privileges that we have as followers of Jesus. This is where the *rubber meets the road.*

I have found that people who come to faith quickly have previously been through the identification and preparation stages with others. I have rarely been present throughout all three stages of their process. On the other hand, I have been used to plant the seed of the Gospel while others have harvested the crop. When God is bringing the hearts of people to receive Jesus, He often uses many people in each stage.

I like to think of sharing the Gospel as an invitation and not an ultimatum. One day, each person will stand before God to be judged. God is the only One Who can judge rightly the heart of each person. Our responsibility is to make sure that people hear the Gospel clearly and that they have an opportunity to respond.

There is only one message that we preach: Paul said that he proclaimed Christ and Him crucified (1 Corinthians 2:2). This is the Good News of Jesus.

I remember years ago sharing my faith with a friend who said he would go home and pray to become a Christian. When I asked him afterwards how it went, he told me that he promised God that he would read the Bible. Reading the Bible is good—in fact it is great!—but reading the Bible does not mean you are a Christian. He clearly didn't understand the message of salvation.

People who have come to our Alpha Course often need the Gospel explained at a personal level. I have often wondered why people don't understand the message because the Alpha Course presents the Gospel so clearly. But sometimes it takes time to process and understand what is being said.

There are often spiritual "blinders" hindering the insight of people who resist the Gospel. In 2 Corinthians we read:

> But even if our Gospel is veiled, it is veiled to those who are perishing, whose minds the god of this age has blinded, who do not believe, lest the light of the Gospel of the glory of Christ, who is the image of God, should shine on them. For we do not preach ourselves, but Christ Jesus the LORD, and ourselves your bondservants for Jesus' sake.
>
> —2 Corinthians 4:3–5

I remember asking one attendee who had completed the entire Alpha Course asking, "Do you know what it means to be 'born-again?'" She stared at me and without any hesitation said, "I haven't got a clue!" We opened the third chapter of the Gospel of John and I explained to her what we mean by the *new birth* or what we commonly call being "born-again."

Once our Alpha Group watched the video entitled *How can I be sure of my faith?* which speaks about the assurance of eternal life for the believer. After it was over, I asked the group if they had heard or understood this message before? One couple blurted out, simultaneously, "I have never heard or understood this message before." These people had a nominal church background but had never heard the Gospel. Another man who had grown up in the church said he learned more about Christianity in three weeks at the Alpha Course than he had in his entire life.

These are just a couple of examples of why we must not assume people know about the Gospel of Jesus Christ. God purposely made the message of salvation simple. In fact, the simplicity of the message of salvation has often been a stumbling block for intellectuals. First Corinthians 1:23 says, "but we preach Christ crucified, to the Jews a stumbling block and to the Greeks foolishness."

The Gospel can be a stumbling block, but make sure people are stumbling over the Gospel—*and not over you!* If people are offended by our behavior or attitude, that is an unnecessary offence, and we must repent and change. If the Gospel is offensive to them, it is accomplishing what God intended. We should bear the reproach of the Gospel willingly, but we should make sure that we are not the source of the reproach.

The command to cry or to preach the Gospel intimidates me. I have had to deal with a strong fear of man. When you are challenged to share the Gospel, you quickly become aware of just how much fear you have! What a slave to the opinions of others I have been! But, no matter how I feel, the command to proclaim the Gospel remains. By my own admission I have not always been faithful to this mandate. I have choked as fear of others overtook me. I have been afraid of rejection. I have even been afraid of physical harm. My problem was that I valued man's opinion more than God's. This area remains a battle for me where I still have to consciously choose to please God rather than man.

When I trust God and share my faith, I am often surprised by a positive response. People are often curious about what and why you believe. It is not our job to save people; that is God's business. Our business is to bear witness (John 1:7). Even when I have been rejected, it has not been as bad as I had expected because God gave me grace to endure the immediate rebuff. I also know that God may be at work beneath a harsh exterior.

Jesus teaches us that bearing shame for His name is an honor (Matthew 5:12). Something very special happens when you share your faith, and the message and messenger are rejected. The Bible says that "If you are reproached for the name of Christ, blessed are you, for the Spirit of glory and of God rests upon you. On their part He is blasphemed, but on your part He is glorified" (1 Peter 4:14–15).

Reinhard Bonnke is a German evangelist who has brought millions to Christ in Africa and around the world. God has used him mightily, but his life is no cakewalk, and he is often criticized by the media. His response is that he is on his International Harvester for Jesus, and he is not stopping for a squeaky mouse! Reinhard has the right priorities. He refuses to let criticism distract him from preaching the Gospel.

One could cite examples of many men and women who once had a mighty calling of God on their lives, but became distracted by criticism. Instead of focusing on Jesus and reaching the lost, they wasted energy counterattacking those who criticized them. Their bitterness hindered their ability to minister. Some even fell into sin. Let this be a warning to us—*we must guard our hearts!* Let the naysayers do what they want, we must resolve not to be distracted, but keep our focus on Jesus.

Be bold in sharing your faith. Don't feel threatened or intimidated. Use wisdom because each circumstance may require a different course of action. Above all, let the motivation for sharing your faith be unwavering.

God has used Nicky Gumbel to share the Gospel with millions of people around the world. I like what he says, "We are not to pressurize people, but to persuade them." We don't want to coerce people into making a commitment to Christ. We want to persuade people by presenting the Gospel in a nonthreatening way, and encouraging them to receive Christ.

Nicky suggests that we avoid "intensity" which creates an atmosphere of tension and pressure. People don't make sound decisions under pressure. They will either succumb to the pressure, making a commitment that is not based on faith, or they will bolt.

When we feel pressured, others will sense our anxiety and feel pressured. If we do not feel pressured, they will not feel pressured. The burden of saving others is on God's shoulders. It is our privilege to share the wonderful message with them.

One of the ways I avoid intensity is by using humor. Victor Borge is reported to have said, "Laughter is the shortest distance between two people."[3] Appropriate humor can break down walls between people and release tension. It can create a friendly atmosphere and make sharing easier. People like to laugh.

At the same time, we need to be careful not to offend people with inappropriate jokes. Sarcastic humor can be very offensive, especially if it becomes personal. Don't share jokes that are off color or racist, as this is a terrible witness. Ephesians 5:4 says, "neither filthiness, nor foolish talking, nor coarse jesting, which are not fitting, but rather giving of thanks."

Excessive humor can also be distracting and draw the focus away from the Lord. Humor can be appropriate when we share a funny story that emphasizes a point we are trying to make.

A Jewish friend once asked me why I went to church. I said, "Because I believe Jesus is the Jewish Messiah." The response was, "Well, I no longer consider you Jewish!" You can imagine the tension! I smiled and said, "Well then, you have some nice Gentile friends you never knew you had!" This humor broke the tension and showed my friend that his objection didn't cause me to take offense.

CHAPTER 18

WHAT SHALL I CRY?

Isaiah asks, "What shall I cry?" This a compelling question. Where do we begin to touch the needs of lost humanity? What is our message? There is only one Gospel. Many modern churches are changing the message to accommodate our culture.

They claim the Bible isn't true; it only *contains* truth. The miracles aren't real; they are only moral illustrations. They would say that the miracle of the loaves and fishes is about giving and not a supernatural event that actually happened. Their worst denial is that Jesus did not die for our sins or rise from the dead, but that His life was an example of love and unselfishness.

Paul tells us if Christ did not rise from the dead then we are still in our sins:

> Now if Christ is preached that He has been raised from the dead, how do some among you say that there is no resurrection of the dead? But if there is no resurrection of the dead, then Christ is not risen. And if Christ is not risen, then our

> preaching is empty and your faith is also empty. Yes, and we are found false witnesses of God, because we have testified of God that He raised up Christ, whom He did not raise up—if in fact the dead do not rise. For if the dead do not rise, then Christ is not risen. And if Christ is not risen, your faith is futile; you are still in your sins! Then also those who have fallen asleep in Christ have perished. If in this life only we have hope in Christ, we are of all men the most pitiable.
> —1 Corinthians 15:12–19

The message of the Gospel is eternal. We cannot compromise this message! Every generation needs to hear it—unchanged. Every person needs Jesus Christ. Many modern churches have changed this message, and have thereby denied the faith.

I remember meeting a new Christian who was taking some theology courses at the local university. His professor was a clergyman who denied the miracles of the Bible. My friend was confused, so I had to explain that not all people who call themselves Christians are true believers. We must hold fast to the message of the Gospel!

The Grass Withers

> The grass withers, the flower fades,
> Because the breath of the LORD blows upon it;
> Surely the people are grass.
> The grass withers, the flower fades,
> But the word of our God stands forever.
> —Isaiah 40:7–8

In summary, this text has three main points: First, that life is temporary—"Surely the people are grass." Second, that death is universal—

"The grass withers, the flower fades." Third, that eternal life comes from God's Word—"But the Word of our God stands forever."

Life is Temporary

Life is short. This is what the prophet Moses says about the greatness of God and the brevity of man:

> LORD, You have been our dwelling place in all generations
> Before the mountains were brought forth,
> Or ever You had formed the earth and the world,
> Even from everlasting to everlasting, You are God.
> You turn man to destruction,
> And say, "Return, O children of men."
> For a thousand years in Your sight
> Are like yesterday when it is past,
> And like a watch in the night.
> You carry them away like a flood;
> They are like a sleep.
> In the morning they are like grass, which grows up:
> In the morning it flourishes and grows up;
> In the evening it is cut down and withers.
> —Psalm 90:1–6

Grass grows very quickly. One spring, my wife and I spread grass seed in our backyard, and in a few weeks we had a beautiful lawn. I had to mow the grass frequently and keep it trimmed, or it became very untidy. One year we had a severe drought and within a short time our beautiful lawn turned brown. In fact, it didn't take long for the drought to kill the grass. We eventually put in an irrigation system to keep the lawn watered.

People are like grass. They spring up, then wither. The Gospel message is vital, and we must make the most of the time God gives us because life on earth is short. There is an urgent need for people to hear about Jesus.

Life is short is because of sin. Sin entered the world through Adam and brought death to every human being. Romans states:

> Therefore, just as through one man sin entered the world, and death through sin, and thus death spread to all men, because all sinned—(For until the law sin was in the world, but sin is not imputed when there is no law. Nevertheless death reigned from Adam to Moses, even over those who had not sinned according to the likeness of the transgression of Adam, who is a type of Him who was to come.)
>
> —Romans 5:12–14

Sin can be both voluntary and involuntary. The sin we inherited from Adam wasn't our choice, but following in his footsteps we all choose to sin. One word used to translate *sin* in the Bible means literally "to miss the mark"—like an arrow missing its target. Another word used for sin is *transgression*, which means "to violate a boundary willfully." As human beings, we are guilty of both. I sometimes define *sin* as "selfishness" because this word captures man's preoccupation with himself, and his propensity to make choices independent from God.

The decisions we make on earth will determine our eternal destiny. Once that choice is sealed, it may never be altered. It is a sobering thought that every person will one day stand before God to give account. Our life on earth is short, but it doesn't end here. Every human being has an eternal destiny which will last forever. One day, we will either be with God in our eternal home or we will be separated from God in eternal punishment. It is painful for me to even write these words.

This is why it is so important to understand how fleeting our lives are. This knowledge should change our priorities, because the choices we make during our short life will control our destiny. Paul tells us that all believers will stand before the judgment seat of Christ to be judged for what we have done in this life, whether good or bad.

> Therefore we make it our aim, whether present or absent, to be well pleasing to Him. For we must all appear before the judgment seat of Christ, that each one may receive the things done in the body, according to what he has done, whether good or bad. Knowing, therefore, the terror of the Lord, we persuade men; but we are well known to God, and I also trust are well known in your consciences.
>
> —2 Corinthians 5:9–11

Believers are not going to be judged as to where they will spend eternity. All true believers in the Lord Jesus Christ are going to heaven, but God will reward us according to our works (1 Corinthians 3:9–17). Those things done for Christ, in the right way, with the right motivation, will be rewarded and those things done in the wrong way will be burned. Paul says some people will be saved as one escapes from a fire, but they will have lost everything but their lives. Knowing that God will reward us for faithfulness should motivate us to live lives that are pleasing to Him.

Non-believers will be at a different judgment where they will be judged according to their deeds and receive eternal punishment:

> Then I saw a great white throne and Him who sat on it, from whose face the earth and the heaven fled away. And there was

> found no place for them. And I saw the dead, small and great, standing before God, and books were opened. And another book was opened, which is the Book of Life. And the dead were judged according to their works, by the things, which were written in the books. The sea gave up the dead who were in it, and Death and Hades delivered up the dead who were in them. And they were judged, each one according to his works. Then Death and Hades were cast into the lake of fire. This is the second death. And anyone not found written in the Book of Life was cast into the lake of fire.
>
> —Revelation 20:11–15

Moses wrote this Psalm as a prayer:

> The days of our lives are seventy years;
> And if by reason of strength they are eighty years,
> Yet their boast is only labor and sorrow;
> For it is soon cut off, and we fly away.
> Who knows the power of Your anger?
> For as the fear of You, so is Your wrath.
> So teach us to number our days,
> That we may gain a heart of wisdom.
> —Psalm 90:10–12

Moses recognized the short span of human life, and prayed that we would number our days so we could have a heart of wisdom. The fleeting nature of life can lead to a melancholy attitude like that of the writer of Ecclesiastes who said that life was vanity.

Everything we accumulate in this life will be taken from us in death. Material possessions rarely last even a lifetime. I remember how excited I was when I purchased a new car. It smelled good and drove so nicely, but within four years it had developed mechanical problems and had begun to rust. Today it is in a junk heap!

When my wife and I married and we moved into our home, I bought a little golden retriever for her. We called our dog *Lady*. We never imagined those days would end, but they did. Eventually we had to give Lady away because our children had allergies. When she died, we all grieved. All of life is fleeting.

The good news is that Christ came to give us life—abundant life (John 10:10). One thing we *can* bring to heaven with us is people. I get excited when people accept Christ because I know they are going to heaven! I am happy when God helps them in this life, but I am thrilled that they will spend eternity with God. Heaven is our eternal home; all earthly existence is temporary.

The things we do for Christ in this life and in this world will have eternal rewards in the life to come. Jesus tells us this in Matthew:

> Do not lay up for yourselves treasures on earth, where moth and rust destroy and where thieves break in and steal; but lay up for yourselves treasures in heaven, where neither moth nor rust destroys and where thieves do not break in and steal. For where your treasure is, there your heart will be also.
>
> —Matthew 6:19–21

You have probably heard the old saying, "You can't take it with you!" which implies that when you die, you lose everything. But this is only partially true. You *can* take the riches that come from following Christ, your rewards, with you (1 Corinthians 3:8).

Paul also refers to *crowns*. We are not sure what kind of crowns these will be, but we know that we will rule and reign with Christ in eternity (2 Timothy 2:12). Rewards and crowns will be given to us according to our faithfulness and service to Christ while we were on earth. All true believers will be in heaven but not all true believers will be rewarded to the same degree, because not all of us have been faithful. Second Timothy 2:20 says, "But in a great house there are not only vessels of gold and silver, but also of wood and clay, some for honor and some for dishonor."

Will we be vessels of honor or dishonor? At the judgment seat of Christ all believers will be judged for their deeds; all will be revealed: every thought, word, deed and action. Believers will not be sent to hell, but we will grieve our failures for a brief moment until God wipes away every tear (Revelation 7:17).

There will be no regrets in eternity, but our life on earth is our only opportunity to repent of selfishness and follow Christ with a whole heart. How much money we make, or how big our house is, or how famous we are—all will mean nothing in the light of eternity. Only what Christ has done through us will last.

So thank God when you are convicted of sin! Matthew 5:4 says, "Blessed are those who mourn, for they shall be comforted." It is better to mourn now than later. When God corrects us here on earth, it is for our eternal benefit so we won't be ashamed when He comes.

Philippians 4:1 says, "Therefore, my beloved and longed-for brethren, my joy and crown, so stand fast in the Lord, beloved." Paul wanted people to come to know Christ and grow into the fullness of maturity. We want also to grow into maturity in Christ.

The shortness of life should motivate us to use our lives for His glory—for eternal purposes that will endure. This is our real purpose in life: to love Christ with all our hearts and to share His love with others.

CHAPTER 19

WHEN TO SHARE: DIVINE APPOINTMENTS

People often ask me how I meet the people with whom I share my faith. I must admit that I am amazed myself at the contacts God provides. I have no easy answer, except that God brings people across my path. When I get to know these people, it often leads to conversations about spiritual matters. The key is to be open to God's leading.

Once when I was on vacation, I asked a worker at the resort where we were staying to show me the path to the beach. After she did, I thanked her and finished by saying, "God bless you."

"Are you a pastor?" she asked.

"No, but my brother is," I replied.

"Do you have to be born-again to get to heaven?"

"Yes, you need to be born-again. Are you born-again?

She paused and looked down as if she was troubled. "No," she said.

I had a hard time reading her thoughts. I thought maybe she needed a little explanation so I asked, "Can I explain what "born-again" means?"

She said, "Yes." She looked pensive and expectant, eager to understand.

I explained a simple message of salvation.

While I was speaking, another resort worker joined us and began to listen. I explained what a person must do to be saved, and when I finished, they both received Jesus Christ as Savior!

In 1 Peter 3:15 we read, "Through thick and thin, keep your hearts at attention, in adoration before Christ, your Master. Be ready to speak up and tell anyone who asks why you're living the way you are, and always with the utmost courtesy" (The Message). As we grow in our relationships with Christ, God will give us opportunities to share our faith. It may surprise you, but people *will* ask you about your faith; so you need to be ready to tell them!

In the book of Genesis, Abraham sent his servant Eliezer to find a wife for Isaac. In Genesis 24, he asked God to direct him. Abraham commanded Eliezer to choose a young woman and bring her back as a wife for Isaac.

Eliezer asked for God's direction and blessing. He trusted God for guidance. He prayed that God would lead him to the right woman. When he came to a well, he asked one of the young women to draw water for him. He told God, "If she offers to draw water for my camel as well, then she is the right woman for Isaac." The young woman was Rebekah, the daughter of Bethuel, Abraham's nephew. She not only watered the camel, but she also fulfilled all the requirements that Abraham set out for a bride for Isaac.

Rebekah brought Eliezer to her home, where he was warmly received by her family. Eliezer then explained his mission to bring home a bride for Isaac, son of Abraham. Rebekah and her family agreed to give her hand in marriage to Isaac.

In Genesis 24:26–27, we read Eliezer's response:

> Then the man bowed down his head and worshiped the Lord. And he said, 'Blessed be the Lord God of my master Abraham, who has not forsaken His mercy and His truth toward my master. As for me, being on the way, the Lord led me to the house of my master's brethren.'

When my son Joshua was young he was invited to a friend's home to play and stay for supper. My wife, Diane, asked me to pick him up. While I was driving to their home, the thought crossed my mind that I would be sharing my faith with the father of the little boy. I immediately prayed for God's leading.

When I arrived at their home to pick up Joshua, the father met me at the door and invited me to come in and have a cup of coffee. I accepted the invitation and came into their home.

"Tell me about yourself" he asked. I told him that I worked in our family real estate business, which my father had started. I explained that our company develops and manages residential and commercial properties. He was new to our city so this gave him an opportunity to get to know me.

He recognized that my name is Jewish, so he asked, "Which synagogue do you belong to?"

"I belong to a church."

"A church?" He asked, obviously surprised. "Aren't you Jewish?"

"Yes, I am," I replied.

"Then why do you go to church?" he asked, quite perplexed.

"I believed that Jesus Christ is the Jewish Messiah!" That led to quite a lively conversation. We have been good friends ever since.

This is just one example of the many situations where I have had an opportunity to meet people and share my faith. Being Jewish gives me an advantage. People are naturally curious to know why I believe in Jesus, because this violates traditional Jewish belief. However, my faith in Christ can pose other problems because the questioner may be hostile!

Our behavior often intrigues people. Matthew 5:16 says, "Let your light so shine before men, that they may see your good works and glorify your Father in heaven."

I met one gentleman, a restaurant owner, and one day when he wasn't overly busy, we had a friendly chat. A week later I was buying some food at his restaurant and he asked me if I liked to play golf. I told him that I didn't like golf (I do now). He then asked if we could have coffee some time and I agreed. He bent over the cash register and said to me in a low voice, "I want to have what you have!" I knew instinctively it wasn't my sense of humor. The next day he came up to see me in my office, shared his heart with me and asked me how to get the peace that I had. I shared with him salvation through Jesus Christ. He then prayed and asked Jesus Christ into his heart! I spoke with him several days later and he told me that he now had the peace that he had seen in me.

Sometimes our behavior is counterproductive. Many people have turned away from the Gospel because of the poor witness and lifestyle of Christians. Because I am a Jewish believer in Christ, many Jewish people have expressed their disillusionment over the horrible way Christians have treated Jews through the ages. This history of poor treatment can create stumbling blocks to sharing our faith.

Several years ago, I was having lunch with a Jewish man who attended synagogue regularly. He asked me to lunch and immediately inquired about my faith. He asked me why Christianity had such a bad track record in its treatment of the Jews. If Christianity were truth, then why did Christ's followers behave so badly? Did that mean that Christianity didn't work? How could it be true if its followers blatantly violated its principles?

I told him that I couldn't justify or explain the actions of other "Christians," but I shared my story with him. I shared why I believed that Jesus Christ was the Jewish Messiah and how His life had changed mine. When I finished, he grabbed my arm and said, "Pray for me and pray hard, I want to have what you have!" This was the heart cry of a man hungry for God.

We need to pray for God to lead us and to give us divine appointments every day. We may not be able to speak openly about our faith in Jesus Christ but our actions speak louder than words. This was echoed by Saint Francis of Assisi who said, "Always preach the Gospel. When necessary, use words." Our lives speak volumes—sometimes louder than our words.

Peter told wives who have unbelieving husbands to win them by their godly behavior, because that would carry more weight than words.

> Wives, likewise, *be* submissive to your own husbands, that even if some do not obey the word, they, without a word, may be won by the conduct of their wives, when they observe your chaste conduct *accompanied* by fear. —1 Peter 3:1–2

Love That Draws Them

The first principle of evangelism is to "speak to the heart." This means getting to know people who are outside the faith and demonstrating unconditional love to them. It means developing a "hearing heart." When we listen to other's needs and bring them before God in prayer we can draw them to Jesus.

We must have a genuine love for others that is *demonstrated* by our behavior toward them. They must feel secure and not threatened. We should not be pushy and demanding. This does not mean that there aren't issues that need to be addressed; it means that God is the one who brings conviction of sin. Romans 2:4 says, "Or do you despise the riches of His goodness, forbearance, and long-suffering, not knowing that the goodness of God leads you to repentance?"

As we earn the trust of others, we can establish genuine friendships with them. We can learn to know them and find common interests. Sports or hobbies can be a great way to get to know people. I often share my business interests with others, and find that meeting people through business often leads to lunches where I have an opportunity to share my faith.

The key is building relationships. Look for common interests that will enable you to direct the conversation toward spiritual matters. Pray for divine appointments and trust God to bring people into your life. Be open. It is God who accomplishes the work. Be sensitive to people's needs, and sensitive to the leading of the Holy Spirit. He will give you the words and the wisdom.

CHAPTER 20

DISCUSSING DEATH

Life is short; death is certain. Many people fear death, and this is why most religions have some belief in an afterlife. Some believe that life ends in death and others hint at a life beyond the grave. Death is a fearful thing for most of us because it is an unknown. We all die and what happens after we die will last forever. It is important to prepare ourselves for death because those decisions have eternal consequences.

Overcoming the Fear of Death

> Inasmuch then as the children have partaken of flesh and blood, He Himself likewise shared in the same, that through death He might destroy him who had the power of death, that is, the devil, and release those who through fear of death were all their lifetime subject to bondage.
> —Hebrews 2:14–15

Jesus has released us from the bondage and fear of death. When we receive Jesus as our Savior, we pass from death to life. John 5:24 says, "Most assuredly, I say to you, he who hears My word and believes in Him who sent Me has everlasting life, and shall not come into judgment, but has passed from death into life."

The moment we accept Jesus Christ as Lord and Savior, we die to our old selves (Romans 6:5–11) and become new creations (2 Corinthians 5:17). Death no longer has power over us because we have already died with Christ. We still suffer *physical* death because flesh and blood cannot inherit the kingdom of God (1 Corinthians 15:50). That is why Jesus refers to this experience as the "new birth" (John 3:3). We are reborn spiritually into a new life.

God's Assurance of Salvation

We can have the assurance of salvation now. What a glorious revelation! We don't have to wait until we die physically to know if we are going to heaven. That is why Paul tells us that today is the day of salvation (2 Corinthians 6:2). Today we can know and experience the salvation of the Lord. I have asked many people if they know they are going to heaven. I often hear, "I don't know but I hope so." As believers in Jesus, we can have *absolute assurance of our salvation*. Why? Because the Word of God tells us we can.

God wants us to be completely free from the fear of death. This freedom from fear attracts those outside the faith! Death is not the final destiny of man. There *is* life beyond the grave. What we have now is scarcely a shadow compared to what is to come. The present earth is our temporary home. Heaven is our eternal home. We are just pilgrims and strangers passing through (1 Peter 2:11).

What our eternal home in heaven will be like is still a mystery, but the certainty of heaven's existence is guaranteed. First Corinthians 2:9 says, "But as it is written: Eye has not seen, nor ear heard, nor have entered into the heart of man, the things which God has prepared for those who love Him." God has given us beauty and nature in this life as a foretaste of the things to come. What we have here on earth cannot be compared to the glorious fullness we will experience ultimately. We live for this new world, and it is into this new world that we invite others.

What Happens at Death?

Paul tells us that to be absent from the body is to be present with the Lord (1 Corinthians 5:3). He wanted to be with the Lord, but he knew that he had not yet finished his earthly mission of helping believers to grow in their faith.

> For to me, to live is Christ, and to die is gain. But if I live on in the flesh, this will mean fruit from my labor; yet what I shall choose I cannot tell. For I am hard-pressed between the two, having a desire to depart and be with Christ, which is far better. Nevertheless to remain in the flesh is more needful for you. And being confident of this, I know that I shall remain and continue with you all for your progress and joy of faith, that your rejoicing for me may be more abundant in Jesus Christ by my coming to you again.
> —Philippians 1:21–26

Paul did not fear death, because he looked forward to being with his Lord—which was far better. He wanted his life to glorify God, and he wanted to finish the tasks for which God created him. Everything—except what we do for God—is temporary and will pass away. God can be glorified even in the most mundane things in life, *if* we purpose to do them for His glory.

> Bondservants, obey in all things your masters according to the flesh, not with eyeservice, as men-pleasers, but in sincerity of heart, fearing God. And whatever you do, do it heartily, as to the LORD and not to men, knowing that from the LORD you will receive the reward of the inheritance; for you serve the LORD Christ. But he who does wrong will be repaid for what he has done, and there is no partiality.
>
> —Colossians 3:22–25

Did you notice the expression "whatever you do?" In everything God can be glorified. We don't have to be in full-time ministry to serve the Lord. We can serve the Lord wherever we are, even in a mundane job. Notice that Paul tells us not to be man-pleasers—individuals who work hard while the boss notices, and stop when he isn't around. Such persons are motivated by man's praise rather than God's praise.

Our purpose should be to serve God and not to seek the recognition of others. When we work hard and no one notices, we are being tested. If we are serving God, then we won't mind! We may even prefer not to be noticed—*because we will be rewarded by God!* Even a cup of cold water in the name of Jesus will earn a reward (Matthew 10:42). Jeremiah prophesied to Baruch, the son of Neriah, and warned him, "And do you seek great things for yourself? Do not seek them." (Jeremiah 45:5). We must stay focused on the Lord.

Too many of God's chosen servants have been distracted by success, and this has caused their ministries to fall. I remember many years ago hearing Derek Prince, an internationally recognized Bible teacher, say that very few Christians can handle the temptation of success; God has to withhold it because of their inability to cope with it in a godly manner. Natural prosperity and success can often keep us lukewarm and spiritually blind unless we keep our eyes and priorities on the Lord (Revelation 3:17).

The Word of our God Stands Forever

What a wonderful contrast! Life is short and death is sure, but God's Word is eternal.

> Since you have purified your souls in obeying the truth through the Spirit in sincere love of the brethren, love one another fervently with a pure heart, having been born again, not of corruptible seed but incorruptible, through the word of God which lives and abides forever, because
>
> All flesh is as grass,
> And all the glory of man as the flower of the grass.
> The grass withers,
> And its flower falls away,
> But the Word of the LORD endures forever.
> —1 Peter 1:22–25

Peter quotes the text from Isaiah 40:8, saying, "Now this is the Word which by the Gospel was preached to you." He is saying that the Word of the Lord that endures forever is the Gospel. The Gospel is our one true hope and assurance of eternal life. It is the eternal, unchanging message of Jesus Christ.

The Gospel of John refers to Jesus as "the Word," who was with God in the beginning and who was God (John 1:1–2). Jesus *is* the eternal Word, and it is His life that we receive. He gave up His life for us— exchanging His life for our life—and longs for us to exchange our life for His! That is why Jesus Christ is referred to as the *liv-*

ing Word. The *written Word*—the Bible—bears witness to the living Word, who is Jesus. John 5:39 says, "You search the Scriptures, for in them you think you have eternal life; and these are they which testify of Me."

CHAPTER 21

DISCUSSING ETERNAL LIFE

We have affirmed that life is short and death is sure, and that the only way to receive eternal life is through Jesus Christ. When explaining the Gospel to people, the simpler the presentation, the more effective. Steps to receiving Christ can be summarized in the following ways:

1) We are all sinners. We are guilty before a holy God and deserve the consequences of eternal punishment. Romans 3:23 says, "for all have sinned and fall short of the glory of God."

2) We must believe that Jesus Christ, God's Son, died on the Cross for our sins; that He rose from the dead after three days in the grave and He has returned to His Father. John 3:16 says, "For God so loved the world that He gave His only begotten Son, that whoever believes in Him should not perish but have everlasting life."

3) We must choose to receive the gift of eternal life by placing our faith in Christ. This means we turn from our sin and we turn to God

and ask Him to forgive us for all our sins and surrender our lives to Jesus Christ. Ephesians 2:8 says, "For by grace you have been saved through faith, and that not of yourselves; it is the gift of God."

We must understand that no one could ever be good enough to earn God's approval through good works. The only way to be saved is by grace, through faith in Christ. Good works don't cut it. Jesus provides everything we need to be saved from eternal separation from God.

Although salvation is a free gift, not everyone is saved because *we must choose to receive it.* We can choose either to accept or reject God's gift of salvation. While we are alive the offer stands, but when we die, the books are closed and we must face judgment before God.

When people are ready to receive Jesus Christ as Savior, I find praying with them is helpful. Remember, it is not a prayer that saves them; it is heartfelt faith. If they do not have faith to receive Christ, then reciting a prayer means nothing. Make sure they are ready to pray to receive Jesus and not under pressure or compulsion to do so.

The Gospel is God's unchanging truth for mankind. God has not and will not present any other plan. The message is changeless and ageless, but the way we share the Gospel is relative. We are talking about communication. If we speak in English to someone who only understands Spanish, there can be no communication. It doesn't matter how sincere we are or how pure our motives; we cannot communicate unless we speak the same language. We must communicate the Gospel in such a way that those to whom we speak can understand what we are saying.

> For though I am free from all men, I have made myself a servant to all, that I might win the more; and to the Jews I became as a Jew, that I might win Jews; to those who are under the law, as under the law, that I might win those who are under the

> law; to those who are without law, as without law (not being without law toward God, but under law toward Christ), that I might win those who are without law; to the weak I became as weak, that I might win the weak. I have become all things to all men, that I might by all means save some.
>
> —1 Corinthians 9:19–22

To communicate the Gospel effectively, Paul had to present Christ in the *context of those who were listening.* If we share the Gospel with individuals who do not understand what we are saying, we have failed to be effective witnesses for Christ. Paul said he came as a Jew that he might win Jews. Paul could come as a Jew because he was a Jew. He wasn't being dishonest or misrepresenting himself; he was genuine. Paul wasn't compromising; he was accommodating. He contextualized the Gospel so that his hearers could understand his message.

My Jewish friends are surprised when I tell them that I still am Jewish even though I believe in Jesus. Rabbinic Judaism rejects Jesus as Messiah and considers Jews who believe in Jesus as apostate. Not all Jews share this view, but many do.

In my view, a Jew who comes to faith in Jesus has not denied his Jewishness but has fulfilled it. Jesus is indeed the Messiah of Israel as well as the Savior of the Gentiles. Romans 2:28–29 tells us that outward appearance alone doesn't make one Jewish; it is the "inward circumcision of the heart" by faith in Jesus Christ that accomplishes this.

This view gives me opportunities to share why I believe that Jesus is the Messiah. Even though my Jewish friends may disagree, it begins a great dialogue about faith!

When I speak to Jews about the Gospel of Christ, I explain the Jewishness of Jesus—His fulfillment of Scriptures and His heart for the

Jewish people. I point them to all the references in the Hebrew Bible that show Jesus is the Messiah. His life, His death, and His salvation for all mankind are all clearly described in passages written by ancient Jewish prophets such as Isaiah. I also explain to them how Jesus fulfilled the Passover. Paul tells us that the Gospel began with the Jews (Romans 1:16.) I tell them that Jewish Christians still remain Jewish—they don't lose their ethnic or cultural identity. God's purpose for Israel and the Jewish people is fulfilled in Christ.

When I share my faith with non-Jewish friends, I normally don't talk about Jewish feasts or customs because these are meaningless to most non-Jews. Gentiles are very curious as to why I believe in Jesus, but I share with them in a different context. I am delighted that I can share the reality of Christ in my life—with both Jews and Gentiles.

CHAPTER 22

THE GOSPEL IS RELEVANT

> Jesus said to him, "I am the way, the truth, and the life. No one comes to the Father except through Me."
> —John 14:6

Remember the three "Rs"? Reading, 'riting, and 'rithmetic? When I was growing up, they were considered the fundamentals of a good education. There are also three *Rs* for communicating the Gospel. Our presentations have to be *relevant*, *real* and *relational* because Jesus Christ is all three.

Jesus is the Way—the Gospel's Relevancy

The Gospel is relevant to our lives. It is God's guidebook to life. Because God knows how to solve our problems, we can apply His truths to our lives with confidence. My friend, Kevin, came to Christ when he realized that God had the answers to the problems he was having with the principal at his school.

Many people think that the Bible is a book of myths. They believe the stories are untrue, and regard people who believe such things to be unscientific, gullible and superstitious. So when educated, respectable, and credible Christians come along, it challenges their false view of the Gospel. I have seen many skeptics change their minds when they see a *reasonable* presentation of the Gospel.

Some people grow up in a religious tradition believing the Bible and the Gospel to be true but boring and therefore do not commit their lives to Christ. When presenting the Gospel we must show that Christ is relevant for people *today*. Methods that worked well a hundred years ago may not be effective today. Singing the old hymns is wonderful in churches where people know them, but trying to reach today's unchurched youth culture with old hymns will not draw them—*it will drive them away!*

A good example of presenting the relevancy of the Gospel comes from the book of Acts:

> Then Paul stood in the midst of the Areopagus and said, "Men of Athens, I perceive that in all things you are very religious; for as I was passing through and considering the objects of your worship, I even found an altar with this inscription:
>
> TO THE UNKNOWN GOD.
>
> Therefore, the One whom you worship without knowing, Him I proclaim to you."
> —Acts 17:22–23

Paul used culturally appropriate illustrations to present the Gospel to his audience. Paul also quoted from the Greek poets so his audience could understand his message (Acts 17:28). Certainly Paul didn't compromise the message; but he did contextualize it. As a result, some people mocked the message, some inquired further, but some believed (Acts 17:32–34).

In every culture and with every age group there is some point of connection that we can use to share the Gospel of Jesus Christ. My friend Dave Overholt is pastor of an inner city youth-orientated church in Hamilton, Ontario, Canada called Church on the Rock. The church's name is a play on words because the *Rock* is Christ, but the youth culture is into contemporary music—and do his services ever rock! As in many churches today, he doesn't wear a clerical collar or a suit and tie, but rather blue jeans and an open-collared shirt. He leads worship with an electric guitar and has a band with drums, bass guitar, and background vocalists. He uses a PowerPoint presentation complete with music videos and slides. I have been to his meetings where one thousand young people worshiped Jesus with arms raised!

He keeps his message under forty-five minutes and always shares the Gospel using language that is understood by his listeners. He speaks of the need for repentance and a changed life, about the reality of Christ to bring hope and deliverance from drugs. He talks about the need for purity, and the radical inward change that Christ produces. He is bringing many young people to Christ and seeing many transformed lives. He is calling the youth to be a "Joshua generation" of believers—meaning that they need to be like the Hebrew generation that went into the Promised Land. He runs discipleship and training courses so that new believers can grow in their faith and reach out to the lost. He is a fantastic youth evangelist—just don't send him to minister in a nursing home!

This is just one example of how the Gospel has been made relevant so that listeners can hear the message not only with their ears but with their hearts. Youth culture has changed over the years. When the hippie movement was strong, "Jesus people" ministered in a way that was relevant to that generation. So while the methods have changed, the message is still the same—Jesus Christ is the Way—the way to peace with God.

CHAPTER 23

THE GOSPEL IS REAL

Jesus is the Truth

I remember sharing the Gospel with a friend who felt, as many people do, that "truth" was subjective and not objective. He believed that what is true for one person is not true for everyone. To him, truth is like time. When it is 2:00 P.M. in New York City, it is also 9:00 P.M. in Jerusalem. The 2:00 P.M. time applies only to people living in the eastern standard time zone. This example illustrates *subjective* truth. However, you cannot apply this theory to the laws of gravity. If you jump off a twenty-story building, you will fall to the ground whether you are in New York or Jerusalem. This example illustrates *objective* truth. The truth about God is objective; it is universal and true for everyone.

God's Word Is True

The objective reality I experience in Jesus Christ is founded in the Scriptures. I believe that the Holy Bible is the foundation for all truth.

We know what truth *is* because of what the Bible *says*. I believe the Bible is true for several reasons.

The first reason I believe the Bible is true is because it describes the human condition so accurately. The characters in the Bible are portrayed honestly with all their human faults and frailties. David was a lover of God, but also an adulterer and murderer. Abraham lied about his wife. Solomon loved many wives, and eventually fell into idolatry. But there were good qualities in their characters as well. The Bible doesn't whitewash their failures but presents them in all their humanity.

A second reason I believe the Bible is true is that it contains practical wisdom about relationships, raising children, dealing with people, honesty, integrity, and life. It presents high moral standards. It teaches us how we should treat one another—with respect and dignity. It teaches us how to love other people and to care for the poor and the helpless. When I follow the Bible, my relationships are healthy. It brings new life to my life.

A third reason I believe the Bible is true is that it is set in a framework of time. The people, places and events are real and historically accurate. We have historical evidence of the Bible's authenticity. It is not mythology; it is describes reality. The Bible is not "once upon a time"; but fixed firmly in time, space and geographic location.

Archeological documents from the Middle East show that an ancient Hebrew civilization existed. Archeologists have located the ruins of biblical places such as Jericho, Ur, Megiddo and many others. There are inscriptions in ancient Hebrew which speak of the God of Israel. Although there are too many finds to mention here specifically, these have become a distinct discipline of study, with excellent resources and study materials available.[4]

A fourth reason I believe the Bible is true is that it contains many prophecies which have been undeniably fulfilled. The Bible predicted many events years or centuries in advance. Jesus Christ accurately fulfilled the Old Testament prophecies such as the place of the Savior's birth (Micah 5:2), and the detailed description of His life and death (Psalm 22 and Isaiah 52:13–53:12). All of these references were fulfilled by Jesus—the only person in history to do so.

A fifth reason I believe the Bible is true is that it is the only book that assures me of eternal life. Most religions are based on human achievement, quite apart from grace. Jesus Christ promises us eternal life by the new birth received by faith, so our eternal existence is not based on our performance.

This understanding takes me back to my teenage years, when I first realized that *if it is up to me, I will never be good enough.* If that is true, and I know it is, then any religion that depends on good behavior to be reconciled with God makes salvation unattainable and to me simply cannot be true.

So I believe the Bible is true because of its historic, moral and prophetic nature. This amazing book leads us into a relationship with Jesus Christ. Simply believing in the Bible will not save us, but the Bible teaches what we must believe to be saved and to live an abundant life.

The Experience of Truth

A second argument which convinces me that Jesus Christ is real is that He can be experienced. We call this experience a relationship with God. I have spoken to "religious" people who don't have *any* relationship with God. Even though they believe in God, they don't *know* Him.

I was once there too, so I appreciate their willingness to admit that they only know about Him; they don't actually *know* Him.

While working on his Master's degree at Princeton University, my friend Leonard had a vision. In the vision he was in a cave with several other people all of whom claimed that they knew the way out of the cave. There was only one problem. They all disagreed on which way was the right way. Leonard is from the deep South, where people have gotten lost in caves with fatal consequences. In his vision, several members of the group were screaming that they knew the way out, but the others disputed their directions. One of the trapped individuals said quietly, "I know the way out." He was not screaming or trying to be convincing but in his quiet demeanor he was quite disarming. He held in his hand a pear with its stem and leaf still attached. Leonard knew instinctively that person knew the way out. Why? The person with the piece of fruit had actually been outside the cave.

Jesus said, "You shall know them by their fruit" (Matthew 7:20). We know the reality of the Gospel of Jesus Christ by the fruit it produces in a person's life. The fruit speaks of the person's character. Galatians 5:22–23 says, "But the fruit of the Spirit is love, joy, peace, long-suffering, kindness, goodness, faithfulness, gentleness, self-control. Against such there is no law."

Several years ago my wife and I started an Alpha Course in our home. One evening after the program was over, a lady stayed behind and asked for prayer to receive Jesus. While we prayed, my friend Derek had a vision for her, in which he saw a zebra. He quietly shared the vision with me afterward and I felt it meant that God was bringing clarity to her life—black versus white—and freedom, because a zebra is a free animal, not domesticated. When we shared the vision with her she was overjoyed because clarity and freedom were what she had been seeking for many years.

The next week when our Alpha group met, the ladies around the dinner table commented that she looked "different." She had an undeniable glow that everyone noticed but couldn't describe. One lady asked if she had gotten her hair cut, but she replied, "No." Another asked if she was wearing a new outfit, and again she said, "No." Finally another person said, "It's your eyes, there is something different about your eyes!" She finally confessed that she had received Jesus the previous week, and her life had been changed. She had a new faith and a new joy! It was evident to everyone and she was thrilled. She has continued to let her light shine as she shares her faith with others.

Jesus is the same yesterday today and forever (Hebrews 13:8). He is still changing people's lives—people from every tongue, tribe and nation (Revelation 7:9). This is what it means to know Jesus as the truth.

CHAPTER 24

THE GOSPEL IS RELATIONAL

Jesus is the Life

My Dad used to say, "People need people." God did not make us to go through life alone. Some people are more private than others, yet we all need other people in our lives. What is true on a *horizontal* plane is even truer on a *vertical* plane. Most of all people need God!

I like to think of the concept this way: The cross of Jesus Christ has two beams, the vertical one represents people reconciled to God; and the horizontal beam represents people reconciled to each other. It's interesting to note that the vertical beam is longer, implying that only when our relationship with God is established, will our relationships with others be healthy and fulfilling.

Our Vertical Relationship

> Then the Lord God took the man and put him in the Garden of Eden to tend and keep it. And the Lord God commanded the man, saying, "Of every tree of the garden you may freely eat;

> but of the tree of the knowledge of good and evil you shall not eat, for in the day that you eat of it you shall surely die."
> —Genesis 2:15–17

The most important relationship we will ever have in life is with God. All earthly relationships are temporary. Loved ones die. Friends move away. Friendships end. Children grow up, get married and have lives of their own. Life on earth is full of change—but the one constant in life is God. He is always there, and always available. When Adam and Eve sinned against God, although they were still physically alive, they died spiritually. When we come to faith in Jesus Christ, our relationship with God is restored through the cross. Ephesians 2:1, 4–5 says:

> And you He made alive, who were dead in trespasses and sins . . . But God, who is rich in mercy, because of His great love with which He loved us, even when we were dead in trespasses, made us alive together with Christ (by grace you have been saved) . . .

When Adam sinned against God in the Garden of Eden—the moment he ate the forbidden fruit—he died spiritually and brought spiritual death to mankind, even though he did not die physically for another nine hundred years. Spiritual death is the death of a relationship, just as divorce is the death of a marriage.

How Christ Restored our Relationship with God

> But God demonstrates His own love toward us, in that while we were still sinners, Christ died for us. Much more then, having now been justified by His blood, we shall be saved from wrath

> through Him. For if when we were enemies we were reconciled to God through the death of His Son, much more, having been reconciled, we shall be saved by His life. And not only that, but we also rejoice in God through our LORD Jesus Christ, through whom we have now received the reconciliation.
>
> —Romans 5:8–11

Jesus Christ reconciled our relationship with God and the result is that we are saved from death. His life becomes our life. When Jesus claims to be the Life, He is claiming it literally, not figuratively. When we receive Jesus Christ as our Savior, He comes to live within us by His Spirit (Romans 8:9). That is the *new birth* (John 3:3). As newborn children of God we are adopted into His family, and He not only forgives our sins but He places a new nature within us (2 Corinthians 5:17).

We become new creations by rebirth. That is how God changes us from the inside out. His Spirit continues to work in our lives after the rebirth by convicting us of sin and revealing more and more of Jesus to us. This is why it is so important not to grieve the Holy Spirit, because that limits His effectiveness in our lives. We are not yet perfect in our behavior but we are being perfected by God, a process known as *sanctification*.

When we accept Christ as our Savior we are instantly *justified*, and in right standing with God. God now sees us through the shed blood of Jesus and has removed the penalty of sin. Our character, however, needs to be changed to reflect the likeness of Christ. This takes time and will not be completed in this life but only in the next life—in heaven. We will never exhibit perfect behavior while we are on earth, but we can allow the Spirit to work in us to bring us closer to God—so others can see Him in us.

This new life in Christ makes all the difference. Paul said that he wanted to provoke his countrymen to jealousy, that through their jealousy some might be saved (Romans 11:11). Some of my Jewish friends have even used this exact expression—they say they are jealous of my relationship with God. A daily walk with God is the most powerful witness we can offer the world. Only God is able to produce such profound change in us; the spiritual quality of our lives flows from within us as we walk in the Spirit.

When God moves in our lives, He makes it obvious to others. I have shared stories of God's supernatural works to people outside the faith, and they believe me because the stories ring true. It is God's Spirit bearing witness to the truth, so I don't have to sound convincing—I simply share what happened. This is what Isaiah meant when he said that "all flesh shall see it together" (Isaiah 40:5). Everyone will recognize that which is of God.

Our Horizontal Relationships

> The Messiah has made things up between us so that we're now together on this, both non-Jewish outsiders and Jewish insiders. He tore down the wall we used to keep each other at a distance. He repealed the law code that had become so clogged with fine print and footnotes that it hindered more than it helped. Then he started over. Instead of continuing with two groups of people separated by centuries of animosity and suspicion, he created a new kind of human being, a fresh start for everybody.
>
> Christ brought us together through his death on the cross. The Cross got us to embrace, and that was the end of the hostility. Christ came and preached peace to you outsiders and peace

> to us insiders. He treated us as equals, and so made us equals. Through him we both share the same Spirit and have equal access to the Father.
> —Ephesians 2:14–18 The Message

One of the teachers of the law asked Jesus which is the greatest commandment? He replied that it was to love the Lord your God with all your heart, soul, mind, and strength; and to love your neighbor as yourself (Mark 12:28–31). When we are reconciled to God by faith in Jesus Christ, we are born into a new relationship with God, and adopted into the family of God.

God never intended us to be independent "lone rangers" of faith. He gave us spiritual brothers and sisters, mothers and fathers. Psalm 68:6 says, "God sets the solitary in families." Before we had a relationship with Christ we were spiritually separated from others, but now we belong to a spiritual family—the family of God.

God gives us gifts so we can serve others, and leaves us dependent on each other so that we might find completion through them. We call this *body ministry*. In Romans, Chapter 12, Paul lists a series of gifts that God gives to each of His children: teaching, prophesying, encouraging, leading, and giving are just a few of the gifts.

Every gift is used to serve others in the body of Christ. We are not to use the gifts for selfish purposes, but rather to benefit others. Salvation is not just "fire insurance," but the beginning of a new lifelong adventure. God has eternal purposes for the gifts He has given us. We are to use them to serve Him and others. This is called *stewardship*.

When Adam and Eve sinned against God, their sin brought conflict into the world—conflict between people, as well as conflict between humans and God. Human strife grieves the heart of God. Wars, terrorism, murders, divorce, and religious strife are all tragic symptoms of inner conflict between people. Christ died to end this conflict and bring reconciliation and peace into our relationships.

Paul specifically referred to the barriers between Jews and Gentiles. Faith in Jesus Christ breaks down even those barriers and brings reconciliation. This is true not only between Jew and Gentile, but also between men and women, and between other people groups. Ethnic groups once hostile towards each other have been reconciled by their faith in Jesus Christ. This has happened over and over again. All around the world where people receive Christ they are reconciled to each other. It is a beautiful thing to witness.

Several years ago my wife and I were on a tour of Israel. We were traveling with a group of Christians who were meeting with Arab and Jewish believers throughout the land. We arrived at an Arab village where we met with an Arab pastor who shared how God had convicted him many years ago that he did not love the Jews, and that he must repent. He went to the nearby town and sought out a local Messianic Jewish pastor and asked his forgiveness for his attitude and sought to help him and his congregation.

The humility and love of this dear Arab pastor moved us all. Our tour guide was a wonderful Jewish believer in Jesus, and as he listened to this story he realized that his own wounds had affected his attitude toward the Arab people. He publicly asked the Arab pastor to forgive him! The tears flowed freely. Prejudice was broken. Forgiveness was granted and healing occurred. Only unity in Jesus could explain their restored relationship.

Of course this is not always the case because people—even Christians—are free to make their own choices. But when people live under the Lordship of Jesus Christ and walk under the influence of the Holy Spirit, miracles of reconciliation happen.

I have seen impossible marriages restored and families in tremendous conflict find peace, when they humbled themselves and sought forgiveness. Reconciliations like these spring from a vibrant relationship with Jesus Christ! Christ has forgiven us, so we can forgive others (Ephesians 4:32).

There is no question that the Gospel of Jesus Christ changes our attitudes toward other people. We see people in a new light.

> Because of this decision we don't evaluate people by what they have or how they look. We looked at the Messiah that way once and got it all wrong, as you know. We certainly don't look at him that way anymore. Now we look inside, and what we see is that anyone united with the Messiah gets a fresh start, is created new. The old life is gone; a new life burgeons! Look at it!
>
> —2 Corinthians 5:16–17 The Message

God changes our attitudes from the inside out. I tell people that my attitude has had a heavenly blood transfusion from "O negative" to "B positive." This positive attitude often attracts people to Jesus Christ. We live in a negative world and people are attracted to people who are genuinely positive. This is the "God magnet" principle at work.

This Scripture sums it up:

> Now all things *are* of God, who has reconciled us to Himself through Jesus Christ, and has given us the ministry of reconciliation, that is, that God was in Christ reconciling the world to Himself, not imputing their trespasses to them, and has committed to us the word of reconciliation.
>
> —2 Corinthians 5:18–19

CHAPTER 25

HOW TO SHARE YOUR FAITH

We have been reconciled to God through Jesus Christ so we can share this message of reconciliation with others. The Gospel is God's power of salvation to *everyone* who believes (Romans 1:16). The Gospel is *relevant*, *real* and *relational*. Everyone needs Jesus. As we examine methods of sharing the Gospel we are really discussing *how* to present the Gospel as relevant, real and relational.

In the late 1800's a man named William Booth was troubled that the church was apathetic about reaching the lost. He recognized that many churches had become mere social clubs, where very little was being done to address social injustices or reach the lost. Young girls were being forced into prostitution. Alcoholism and poverty were rampant, yet the church did not seem to care.

William Booth began an outreach, which became known as the Salvation Army. He set Christian words to drinking songs—melodies previously sung in taverns. People in the streets heard the songs, recognized the melodies and listened to the new words. William Booth contextualized the Gospel. He grabbed the attention of the people he wanted to reach with effective ministry, which reached the lost and helped those who were down and out. Sadly much of the criticism against him came from within the Church.

This is not surprising because people often resist change—both positive and negative. Back then the churched people were uncomfortable hearing Christian words set to worldly music. This practice seemed ungodly to them because they missed the point of Booth's initiative. He wanted to reach the lost, those who spent their free hours in taverns. He used unconventional methods to reach his target audience. William Booth was not compromising the Gospel but contextualizing it.

A woman once told Dwight L. Moody, a famous American preacher of the nineteenth century, that she did not like his method of evangelizing. When he asked her how she evangelized, she told him that she didn't—it wasn't her gift. Moody told her that he liked his way better than her way.

Others may criticize you when you share the Gospel. Don't allow yourself be distracted by the negative opinions of others. Be faithful to what God has called you to do. I have sometimes been criticized for sharing the Gospel, but I simply remember those who have come to faith, and the criticism, however great, simply fades away.

Let Them Know

> Instead, you must worship Christ as Lord of your life. And if you are asked about your Christian hope, always be ready to explain it.
>
> —1 Peter 3:15 NLT

The first way to evangelize is by simply telling people that you are a Christian. As my friend George Morley says, “Raise your banner of faith!” Don’t be ashamed of being a Christian. You have the greatest message in the world and should never underestimate the power of your testimony.

I look for opportunities to let people know I am a Christian. I don’t force opportunities, but I make my position known. I recognize that I am a co-laborer with Christ. He works out the circumstances, and I respond to them in faith. When I meet people, I understand it is for a purpose.

Last September, I was in my office when I got a call from a Jewish woman who had heard about me from a mutual friend. She came to see me a few days later.

Sharon had been raised in a Jewish home, but for many years had not been active in her faith. The previous winter she had met some Christians, who had piqued her interest in Jesus. She wanted to know why I believed that Jesus is the Messiah.

She asked me if I had heard of the Alpha Course. I told her that I was starting one in my office in two weeks! The timing couldn’t have been better. I asked her if she had heard of Stan Telchin only to learn she had just finished reading his book! I told her that Stan was coming to our church to speak in a few weeks and invited her to come and hear him.

She came to the Alpha Course, and she also came to our church to hear Stan. Stan is a friend of mine and a Jewish believer, whose compelling life story, *Betrayed*, tells how he and his family came to believe in Jesus.

Sharon struggled to reconcile the concept of being Jewish and believing in Jesus. This is common struggle for Jewish people. When she heard Stan's story, she realized that being Jewish and believing in Jesus *were* compatible. But she still needed time to process her decision to follow Christ.

A week later was Yom Kippur, the holiest holiday of the Jewish year. It is a day of devout fasting and repentance, so Sharon was fasting and reading the New Testament. That night she dreamt that Jesus was holding her. The next night, she had the same dream. On the third night, she was awake and felt someone lift her up out of her bed. A bright golden light filled the room. She said, "Lord, I am not afraid, what are you trying to tell me?" The warm light came into her and filled her heart with love and peace.

At that point Sharon surrendered her heart to Jesus. She kept saying, "Thank you God, thank you Jesus." She later prayed with me to confirm her decision to follow Jesus Christ, and to be filled with the Holy Spirit. She has come to know the peace and joy of believing in Jesus Christ.

We should always be ready to give an explanation of the Gospel when asked. I am Jewish, so I am often questioned by people about my faith. I simply tell them why I believe in Jesus Christ. You can do the same. Simply share what you believe with your friends from your own experience.

The Power of Personal Testimony

Your own personal testimony is one of the most powerful tools you possess. Some of the best evangelistic books are those that give a personal account of a life changed by Jesus Christ. If you are a believer in Jesus, then you have a testimony that needs to be shared with the world.

When Jesus met the woman at the well in John, Chapter 4, He had such an impact on her life that she told all the people in the village about the Man who had told her everything that she had ever done.

> And many of the Samaritans of that city believed in Him because of the word of the woman who testified, "He told me all that I ever did." So when the Samaritans had come to Him, they urged Him to stay with them; and He stayed there two days. And many more believed because of His own word.
>
> Then they said to the woman, "Now we believe, not because of what you said, for we ourselves have heard Him and we know that this is indeed the Christ, the Savior of the world."
>
> —John 4:39–42

Because of the woman's testimony, the Samaritans' curiosity was aroused and they came out to meet Jesus. They saw him face-to-face and had their own faith encounters. They did not need second-hand faith; instead they entered into their own relationship with Jesus Christ. It often works that way with us. We share our testimony with others so they can have their own experience and they in turn share their experience with others. Through us, God reproduces His kingdom.

I recommend writing your testimony down on a piece of paper or typing it into your computer. Keep it short. Summarize the main points: why you believed, when you believed, and the circumstances that brought you to faith. Make sure when you share your story that you present the Gospel clearly.

Throughout this book you have heard my personal testimony, but just to give you a sense of how much detail I share with seekers, I am going to give you the version I usually share.

I was raised in a Jewish home with a very strong belief in God. From age seven to eleven, I studied in a private Hebrew Day school where we learned the culture, customs and language of my people. I was proud of my Jewish heritage and loved my Jewish community.

After my Bar Mitzvah at thirteen years of age, I began to look for life's answers. I was no longer happy to just to believe in God, I wanted to know Him. The harder I tried to find God the farther away I felt from Him. I began to realize my own faults, shortcomings and sins. It seemed impossible to bridge the gap between myself and God. I became depressed and questioned whether I would ever be good enough for God.

One day while I was out for a drive with my brother and his two friends, as I was gazing out the window, I said out loud, "I wonder if there is a God?" My brother's friend quickly replied, "There is and I know Him!" I was captivated. I had to know more.

That evening my brother dropped the two of us off at my home and while we were in the basement, Hank explained to me the message of salvation. He explained that Jesus Christ was the Jewish Messiah who died for my sins and the sins of the whole world. I could receive Jesus Christ by faith if I prayed and asked Him to forgive my sins and come into my heart. That night I prayed a prayer with Hank to receive Jesus Christ. I went something like this: *Dear God, I have done wrong things in my life and I can't fix myself. I ask You to forgive me for every wrong thing that I have done. I turn away from my sin and to You. I believe that Jesus Christ Your Son died for my sins on the cross and was raised from the dead. Please come*

> *into my life right now and give me eternal life. I ask this in Jesus' name.*
>
> After I prayed that prayer I felt such joy and peace. I now knew God's love and forgiveness through Jesus Christ.

When you share your story with others, tell people the absolute truth. Don't sensationalize your story. Some people have amazing stories of deliverance from drugs and sin. You may have grown up in a Christian home and church, and have never tasted a drop of alcohol in your life. You may feel that your testimony is boring. That is far from true. People may need to hear how God's power preserved you from the pollution and degradation of sin. Daniel is a Biblical example of such a testimony: the power of God worked in his life to protect him from stumbling.

You may have the opposite testimony. You may have grown up in a Christian home, but turned away and fell into sin. Later, when you came back to faith, you may have felt ashamed of the things you did. However, your story of victory can bring healing and encouragement to others traveling the same path or parents whose children have left the faith. Romans 8:29 says that "All things work together for good for those who love God." This is true in your life and mine.

Keep your testimony simple. Don't try to convince people, just tell them what you have experienced. One of the most beautiful things about the Gospel is its *simplicity*. People make things complicated, but God has made His plan simple. In fact it is so simple even children can understand and receive Jesus Christ as Savior. In sharing, we are not trying to promote ourselves; we are drawing the attention to Jesus.

I have often related God's answers to prayer, or other amazing personal experiences, as I have shared the Good News with others. These stories pique people's interest in God, making them want to hear more. Many people have never understood that they can have a *personal* relationship with God; it has never crossed their mind. So when we share our stories with them, we are not just sharing an experience but we are opening up possibilities for them to explore.

Practice Telling your Story

This may sound mechanical but it is actually very helpful to rehearse our testimonies. Most of us tend to feel shy, awkward and uncomfortable when speaking about personal issues such as faith. When I became a Christian, the first people I shared my faith with were other Christians. It was natural to share with them because I wanted to meet other believers and get to know them.

One of the first things I do when I meet Christians is ask them to tell me about themselves. We often end up sharing our stories with each other. I share my story with Christian friends in exactly the same way I do with non-Christian friends. I don't have two versions. I go through the Gospel message thoroughly because it helps me to practice telling my story. If you make the most of these opportunities, you will become experienced in sharing your story and be more comfortable doing so.

Don't underestimate the power of your personal testimony: it may be the most effective weapon you have in your spiritual arsenal. People are more likely to read your life than to read a Bible! Your behavior and life are going to make a significant impact on people. How you treat your family and your work ethic all play key roles in reaching the lost. People will look at your values when you tell them you are a believer. They will *expect* to see a difference.

My brother, Howard, was meeting with a colleague to discuss an engineering problem. The engineer observed Howard in the work place and noticed that none of the interruptions or responsibilities bothered him. The fellow wondered how Howard could have so much peace in the midst of chaos and conflict, so Howard shared the Gospel of Jesus Christ with this engineer, and he too gave his heart to Christ.

CHAPTER 26

OTHER WAYS TO SHARE YOUR FAITH

People will give you little clues when they are ready to receive Jesus. The questions they ask will often tell you when they're ready. They may ask how their life will change if they accept Christ. Assure them of God's unconditional love and dispel their fears. When they are ready, have them repeat the prayer after you to receive Christ, because most people are unsure of what to pray and are afraid of saying the wrong thing. Praying together can also serve as a precious memory of the day they decided to follow Jesus.

One tool that I use is a tract called the "Bridge to Life," that is published by the Navigators. It is inexpensive and can be purchased at most Christian bookstores. Brief and convenient to use, it explains the Gospel in a simple way using short Scriptures with pictures to illustrate the truth. Most people are visually oriented, and I find this presentation quite helpful. In the back of the booklet there is a prayer for people to receive Christ.

Before praying with people I always ask their permission. They need to be in control of what will be the most important decision in their life! So simply ask, "Would you like me to pray with you to receive Jesus?" It is important to let them know that you respect them, and will still accept them, regardless of their decision. Let them know they matter a great deal to you.

There are many tracts and books available that can be shared with others, but use care because handing out tracts and books can offend some people. One problem with books is that it takes time to read them. If people are motivated and have the time, then books are an excellent resource. Lee Strobel's well-researched book, *The Case for Christ: A Journalist's Personal Investigation of the Evidence for Jesus*, examines the resurrection of Christ. Another of his books, *The Case for Faith*, tackles hard questions such as why human beings suffer. A third book entitled, *The Case for A Creator,* outlines the scientific evidence for a creator. I highly recommend these books for those who are investigating the claims of the Gospel. The books are all the more compelling because Strobel is a legally-trained investigative journalist, who began investigating the claims of Christ with a mission to disprove Christianity—and in the process became a believer.

Some of the most effective books are those that present personal stories. Try to find a testimony of someone with a background similar to the people you are trying to reach. Stan Telchin's book *Betrayed* has sold millions of copies worldwide. I have met many people whose lives have been impacted and changed by his book.

CDs and Videos

People often need time and space to process the information they receive. I have purchased CDs and videos to give to those who need time alone to think about the Gospel message. One excellent CD series is by Dr. Paul L. Maier, a professor of Ancient History at Western Michigan University, titled *Jesus—Legend or Lord*? He looks at the historical Jesus and presents a credible picture of the life, death and resurrection of Jesus Christ.

Alpha lecturer Nicky Gumbel calls the resurrection of Christ the linchpin of Christianity. Our faith hinges on the fact that Jesus rose from the dead. Paul Maier does an excellent job of presenting the Gospel message using both the Bible and historical evidence outside the Bible.

I often give these CDs to people who come to our Alpha Group or to business people who have very little time. When I sense that they are open to the Gospel, I offer them a set of CDs and invite them to have lunch with me in a month's time. In this way, they can listen to the message of Jesus Christ and reflect in the privacy of their car while driving to work.

Videos and DVDs can also be effective but they are more time consuming to watch, and privacy, even in one's home, can be an issue. There are excellent video materials available for those interested in the Gospel. Some of these materials cover topics such as science and faith, evolution versus creationism, raising children in a Christian home, and how to deal with finances as a Christian. Some of these materials may not appear to be evangelistic, but they show Christian solutions to life's questions.

Music

Music universally appeals to the heart of man. Man was created to worship, and I have found that giving CDs and music videos to seekers is a very effective way to open people's hearts to the Gospel message. People long to have a worship experience with God. I remember giving a worship CD to a friend and he said that as he listened to the music, tears flowed down his face. Another friend said that as he watched the video and saw people entering into worship, he was truly jealous of their experience.

Sometimes this hunger for worship leads people to attend a concert or church service so they can experience first hand a touch from the Spirit of God. A Jewish friend of mine attended a church service in response to a friend's invitation. During the service someone spoke in tongues in Hebrew. Because he knew Hebrew, he understood what was being said, but he didn't realize until later that the person speaking did not know Hebrew! God was speaking to him supernaturally. Sometime later, he gave his heart to Christ.

Bibles, New Testaments, and The Gospel of John

Of course the Bible is a powerful tool to bring people to faith in Christ. Gideon International is an organization committed to providing Bibles and New Testaments to schools, hotels and other public places. This organization has been used mightily by God to bring salvation through the distribution of Scripture.

However, the Bible is a long book and can be difficult to understand. If people show any interest in reading the Bible, I often suggest they begin reading the New Testament or the Gospel of John. I recommend a modern translation that is understandable but remains faithful to the meaning of Scripture. There are many modern translations from which to choose. I personally like the *New Living Translation*, because it reads well and has footnotes at the bottom to clarify the meaning of the words.

Copies of the Gospel of John can be purchased fairly inexpensively and are more likely to be read than the whole Bible. The Gospel of John is usually accompanied with an introductory guide that clearly explains the meaning of salvation. Your local Christian bookstore will likely have several different editions from which to choose.

At other times a New Testament or the Gospel of John may not be the best place to begin. Jewish people often prefer the Old Testament. I suggest they read the Messianic prophecies that were fulfilled by Christ using something like Josh McDowell's book, *Evidence that Demands a Verdict*, which lists each prophecy specifically.

CHAPTER 27

THE ALPHA COURSE

Throughout this book I have made many references to the Alpha Course because we have used it so extensively in our home. I will explain how we use this course and how you might use it too. If you are unfamiliar with it, I will share a little background concerning Alpha.

The Alpha Course originated in London, England at Holy Trinity Brompton Anglican Church about twenty-five years ago. It was developed to train new church members in the basics of the Christian faith. Those who were taking the course soon realized that it was a great way to reach those outside the church with the Gospel of Jesus Christ. Around 1993, five other churches in London adopted the Alpha program and soon it spread worldwide. Today over seven million people in almost every major Christian denomination have taken the Alpha Course.

Audiotapes of the course and eventually videotapes and DVDs were produced and used to communicate the Gospel. Some churches prefer to do the Alpha Course with their own presenter. In this instance, the book *Questions of Life* serves as the written guideline for the course and the presenter may use his or her own illustrations. There are many other resources available through Alpha, including training manuals, tapes, and conferences on how to run an Alpha Course. There are national Alpha offices in many countries, with regional coordinators. Leader's guides and discussion booklets are also available. The support and resources provided by Alpha are excellent. More information about Alpha may be found on the Internet.

The materials are updated routinely with minor changes reflecting current events; however, the basic content remains the same. Alpha runs as a ten-week course designed to introduce people to the basics of the Christian faith, and really is a fantastic tool for evangelism and discipleship. Topics covered include: Who Is Jesus? Why Did He Die? How Can I Be Sure of My Faith? How and Why Do We Read The Bible? How and Why Do We Pray? as well as other relevant subjects.

There is a weekend retreat that covers material about the Holy Spirit. Many people are deeply touched by God at the retreats.

Alpha Courses are currently running in churches, homes, prisons, and places of business. We have found the Alpha Course is also a great tool for personal evangelism in the privacy and security of one's home.

The structure of the Alpha Course is the same each week. First a day and time are chosen. Each session begins with a home-cooked meal and delicious desserts, with any dietary restrictions determined in advance. We try to be accommodating so that no one feels excluded from the program. We allow one hour for the meal, so there is time for personal relationships to develop. Providing a meal also saves people time from having to go home, prepare dinner and clean up afterwards, and we found that many come directly to Alpha from their workplaces.

After the meal we watch the video featuring Nicky Gumbel addressing the topic of the evening. The videos run about forty-five minutes in length, are dynamic, fact-filled, and fun to watch. We receive very positive comments each week, even from those who don't agree with the content. Some guests who came out of curiosity the first week have such an enjoyable time that they come back again. Following the video, a small group discussion allows the attendees to share their thoughts about the video.

A group leader facilitates the discussion, but doesn't dominate the group time. He or she will ask leading questions to get things going such as "What did you think of the material?" or "What did you feel about the message?" It is important to let people know that *any* question is appropriate and that there is no such thing as a stupid question. The purpose isn't necessarily to *answer* their questions, but to allow all participants to express themselves. Others in attendance will respond to questions raised and this invariably leads to a healthy group dynamic and discussion.

We provide resource materials such as Bibles, books, tracts, or tapes to anyone who requests them. Our purpose is to encourage them in their search—not to control them. We never use the group time to pressure people, and should someone want to receive Jesus as Savior, this is done privately outside of the group. If people request public prayer, we will oblige, but this is extremely rare. Our desire is to build trust.

When the course is completed, we encourage those who would like to continue to grow spiritually to find a church and a home group. Many who attended initially as guests, return as helpers on the next Alpha Course, or bring friends or relatives. We try to maintain relationships after the Alpha Course is finished so that people feel connected.

How We Became Involved with Alpha

Six years ago I had the privilege of bringing two fellow workers to Christ. We would meet weekly and read the Bible together and have a brief time of prayer. I felt that they needed something more than our time together to grow spiritually. When I mentioned church, they squirmed. They had not grown up in church and did not want to go. I told them that our church offered an Alpha Course and invited them to come with me. I hadn't been to one, but I thought I would go if they were willing, but they both said "no."

I then asked if they would come to the course if I held it in my home. They agreed to think about attending. When I discussed this with my wife, Diane, she said she would love to do an Alpha Course in our home. I didn't realize that we were about to embark on one of the most significant ministries of our lives.

In the fall of 1999, we opened our home to our first Alpha Course. We had over 27 adults and 13 children come to our home for a meal each week. The children had a separate program from the adults. During the first course nine people gave their hearts to Christ! I still remember the first week with people coming and the doorbell ringing and ringing. Terry, one of our guests, looked at me and said, "I thought this was going to be a small group!"

Terry, who works with me, brought his wife, Vicky, and their son Colin. Vicky told Terry that if anyone asked her personal questions, she was going to leave and never come back! We had such a large group that we had to set up three separate discussion groups after the video. Vicky and Terry were in my discussion group. In the discussion group people shared what they believed. One man said he was raised in a home that was basically atheistic and didn't really believe in God. Others shared what they believed. Terry and Vicky were silent until someone asked them, "You aren't saying much, are you atheists? What do you believe?"

Vicky then spoke and told everyone that she was raised in a nominal Christian home. She believed in God and the Ten Commandments but didn't know if she would go to heaven. She hoped she would, but she wasn't sure. She spoke for about ten minutes and by her own admission was surprised that she had done so. Knowing how sensitive she is, I wondered if she would come back the next week.

The next week their son Colin got home from school and immediately did his homework. Then he sat in the car insisting that they go back to our home because he had had such a good time. Colin's persistence melted away Vicky's resistance. After a few weeks, Vicky became more and more comfortable with everyone in the group. She thoroughly enjoyed the Alpha videos and Terry was also having a great time meeting people and learning more about his faith.

At about week five, I could sense that Vicky was ready to pray to accept Christ as her Savior. I asked her if she and Terry could stay for a few minutes after the meeting was over and they agreed. I asked her if was she enjoying the course and she told me that she loved it. I reminded her that when she started the course she was hoping that she was going to go to heaven but wasn't sure. I asked her if she would like to be sure by accepting Christ. She said that she longed for a relationship with Christ so in the privacy of that moment she prayed with her husband and me and received Christ as her Savior.

From that very moment, her life changed, and her husband Terry told me that Vicky had become a brand new person. She was a wonderful person before, but she became a bright light for Jesus Christ, and since that time has been a helper on other Alpha Courses. In fact, she has led others in her family to a personal relationship with Jesus Christ.

The most interesting thing was the impact the Gospel had on their son, Colin. At the time his mother and dad committed their lives to Christ, Colin was eleven years old. One Sunday Vicky decided to attend our church and she brought Colin. Terry had worked late the night before and needed to rest. I invited Vicky and Colin to sit with us, and she was horrified to find herself at the front of the church!

The pastor's sermon was about how God seeks and finds us. To illustrate his point he asked for two children to come up on the platform. Colin went up with another child. Pastor asked them to hide on the platform and then he went looking for them. When he found them he rewarded them with a candy. His point was that God is seeking and saving the lost.

A couple of weeks later Colin had a dream. In his dream he was in another church (one he had never seen before) and was playing musical chairs with other children. There was a pastor organizing the activity.

The next day he was invited by a friend to join their youth group's bowling league. After bowling, the group went to the church and played musical chairs and the pastor was the same man he had seen in the dream!

The next week Colin and his mother came back to our church. On this Sunday our pastor was preaching on how God speaks through dreams and visions. After church, Vicky and Colin came to our house for lunch and we discussed the pastor's message.

Vicky remembered Colin's dream and asked him to share it. Vicky asked us, "What does this mean?" I felt that God was speaking through both the dream and the experience at church. God was seeking after Colin and He had a place for him in the body of Christ. Colin thought that was pretty cool. When I offered to pray with Colin to receive Jesus, he seemed reluctant but when my daughter, Michelle, explained salvation to him, he saw his need. Right there we joined hands together and prayed as Colin committed his heart to Jesus.

Several months later, Colin went to visit his grandfather where he lay dying. Colin explained to him the way of salvation, and was thrilled when his grandpa prayed with him to receive Christ!

Maurice and Pearl

Pearl works with me in the same company and when we offered our first Alpha Course, I invited her to participate. She brought her husband, Maurice, a successful retired businessman, who had been a director of an international company in the West Indies. At the time of this Alpha, Maurice was somewhat skeptical about religion. He later told me that he went along because we were Pearl's co-workers, but he had no real interest in the subject. The material caught him off guard, and by the third week he was convinced that Jesus Christ was the Son of God. I remember the night that he said, "I was not convinced before, but I am now!" Shortly after this he accepted Christ as his Savior along with his wife, Pearl.

Sometime after Maurice accepted Christ, we went out for lunch. He bemoaned the fact that he had found Christ so late in life and felt that his life would have been so different had he met Jesus when he was younger. I told him that God could use him even at this time in his life. He said, "I hope so."

He is now eighty-one and going strong. Since that time, Maurice has introduced Alpha to his friends in Jamaica where he lived for so many years. He is a blazing witness for Christ and has been instrumental in leading many others to the Lord.

In Scripture, Jesus compared the Gospel to yeast in dough:

> "The Kingdom of Heaven is like yeast used by a woman making bread. Even though she used a large amount of flour, the yeast permeated every part of the dough." — Matthew 13:33 NLT

As the Gospel spreads, it expands like yeast. Terry came to Christ at work and his wife came to Christ at the Alpha Course. Their son Colin came to Christ after they began attending church, and Colin led his grandpa to Christ before the elderly man died. This kind of lifestyle evangelism illustrates what it means to be a "God magnet."

Diane and I have just finished running our ninth Alpha Course in our home. We have also helped with two at our church. We have watched over 200 people go through the Alpha Course, and heard many amazing stories. Of course not all of the attendees have come to faith, but we have yet to run an Alpha Course where *someone* hasn't come to faith.

Starting an Alpha Course

God has blessed Alpha Ministries, and there are Alpha Courses almost everywhere. You can find one by logging on to the website at www.alphacourse.org which provides information about local programs and ministry materials. I would suggest finding a local church and joining one of their courses before hosting an Alpha Course for the first time. You might want to invite a friend who is not a Christian, but who wants to find out more about the Christian faith. It is also helpful to read the book *Questions of Life* before you host an Alpha Course. If you are in a non-English speaking community, the website has information about Alpha courses in many different languages.

CHAPTER 28

OTHER TOOLS

Prayer Ministry

While the Alpha Course has been a wonderful blessing to us, and to many others, it is not the only method to bring people to Christ. Many people have found prayer to be an effective evangelism tool. In prayer ministry we do not just pray *for* people but we pray *with* people. Pearl, the lady mentioned previously, came to Christ at our Alpha Course. After she came to Christ she told me that customers were opening up their hearts to her, and she wasn't sure how to respond.

One day a lady wanted to meet with her to ask her about the Lord, and Pearl asked me to join them. When the lady arrived, she poured out her heart and her need for God. I brought out a "Bridge to Life" tract and I explained the way of salvation. I then asked if she would like to pray and accept Christ and she said that she would. In Pearl's office this lady gave her heart to Christ.

On another occasion, Pearl brought an older woman into my office who wanted prayer, then promptly closed the door and left me to deal with the situation. I didn't know what to do next, but the woman shared her problems and she asked me to pray about them. When I explained the Gospel to her and asked her if she would like to receive Jesus, she indicated she would, and right there we prayed together and she became a Christian. She later attended an Alpha Course and began attending a local church.

Responding to people's needs can become an opportunity to share Christ through prayer. It is not always necessary to pray with them at the time. I once found one of our subcontractors lying on the floor in pain. I was shocked and asked him what had happened. He told me that he had a painful degenerated disk in his back.

When I offered to pray for him he sounded offended and declined. Then he changed his mind and asked me to pray for him but not then and there. I prayed for him when I was alone, but my prayer felt weak. My words weren't eloquent, nor did I feel particularly spiritual. In my prayer I asked God to heal him in such a way that he would know it was from God.

I soon forgot about my prayer and went on about my business. The next time I saw him, a year later, he came up to me and asked me if I had prayed for him. I said, "Yes." He said, "Whatever you did worked!" His back was healed even though the doctors' prognosis had been that his condition would deteriorate until he was crippled.

This story shows that we don't have to pray lengthy or eloquent prayers. God answers our prayers because of His grace, not because of our words. Later that week we went for lunch, and I shared the Gospel with him. This time he was keenly interested. I don't know if he ever accepted the Lord but the seed was sown. It is now God's business to bring in the harvest.

Personal Invitations

There is something about the word invitation that is so *inviting!* Suppose you received a personal invitation to dine with the Queen. Or the President! Let us also suppose that the invitation was sent to you alone and was not sent in the mail but was hand delivered to you by their personal emissary. How would you feel? Wouldn't you feel honored? Wouldn't you be thrilled?

When we present others with an opportunity to receive Christ, we are expressing the heart of God. We are the emissaries of our great King Jesus and we are offering people a personal invitation to dine with the King! (Revelation 3:20).

The personal expression of the invitation will depend on the person and that individual's circumstances, so there are no hard and fast rules. Each person needs to know that they are so special that God wants to speak to them individually. It is true that God loves all of humanity, but He also loves each one of us. We are saved individually, and He expresses His love and intimacy to each one of us personally.

So each person must be asked if he or she would like to receive Jesus Christ. If a person comes from a Christian background it may be offensive to say, "Would you like to become a Christian?" They may already think they are a Christian, or feel that you are judging them.

Several years ago, I shared my testimony with a business acquaintance, and then I said, "You may have already prayed to receive Jesus, but can you remember a time when you did?" He told me that the one thing that impressed him with my story was the fact that I had had a *defined experience*, which he had not had; he could not recall a specific time when he had given His life to Christ.

I then asked him if he would like to make sure that he had given his life to Christ. If he had already done so, no harm would be done, but if he wasn't sure, this would confirm his decision to receive Christ. He told me that he would like to receive Christ. I told him that prayer is very personal and sometimes hard to express, and if he wished I would be happy to lead him in a prayer to receive Jesus. He could either use my words or choose his own words. Words are the vehicle by which salvation happens but the most important thing was his willingness to receive Jesus.

This conversation happened over lunch at a restaurant, and I waited until we were back in the privacy of my office to pray with him. He prayed with me to give his life to Christ! This is just one example of how to personally invite people to receive Jesus.

It is important that the person not feel pressured to respond immediately. They may want to think it over, as with any invitation. Recently I asked one our Alpha attendees if she was ready to receive Jesus. She turned to me and said, "Ask me again." In other words she was saying, "Not yet, but soon." Two weeks later she gave her heart to Christ by herself in her own home!

The invitation must be personalized, and it must be sensitive. I find that asking questions and proceeding according to their answers is the best method. For example, "How do you feel about Jesus?" "Can you remember a time when you prayed to receive Jesus?" "Does the message of Jesus make sense to you?" "Can I bring some clarification to the message of Jesus?"

Their response will determine whether or not you should proceed. If they don't understand the message of Jesus, then they are not ready to proceed and we shouldn't try to convince them. It is important to be sensitive to subtle social cues because these are messages that communicate their state of readiness. When someone backs off, it is best not to press them further.

I often tell people that this is an important decision, one that they must make for themselves. If they are not ready, I thank them for listening to me, express my appreciation for them, and let them know that I am always available for them if ever they want to talk. I want them to feel *safe*. At this point, it is most important to be patient. Don't make others feel that they are letting you down; just continue to love them!

The Sinner's Prayer

Even when people are ready to pray, it can be difficult because it is such a personal moment. I always tell them in advance what is involved in saying the sinner's prayer.

This is what I say: These are the key things that we want to cover in prayer:

1) We are going to come before God.

2) We are going to acknowledge that we are not "good enough" to get to heaven by ourselves, and that our sin has separated us from God.

3) We are going to thank God for sending Jesus Christ His Son to die on the cross for our sins and for raising Him from the dead.

4) We are going to ask Him to forgive us for all of our sins.

5) We are going to ask Him to take our life and live through us.

That is the meaning of surrender; we are giving ourselves up to God. Repentance means that we are now looking to God for direction instead of going our own way.

When I finish explaining how and what we are going to pray, I ask if they have any questions and if they are in agreement with the prayer before we proceed. Sometimes the person is alone or sometimes they are with a Christian friend. I ask everyone to pray together so that no one is singled out. It doesn't hurt for others to pray alongside, and it takes away some of the self-consciousness.

A sample prayer is included below. Remember, heartfelt sincerity is more important than the specific words, but the words are important because they express faith. Romans 10:9 says, "that if you confess with your mouth the Lord Jesus and believe in your heart that God has raised Him from the dead, you will be saved."

I try to keep the language simple and clear so that the person can both understand and agree with the prayer. Avoid eloquent language, especially "Christianese" which may be intimidating and make a person just coming to Christ feel inferior.

Here is a sample prayer:

> Dear God, I know that I have sinned against You. I am not good enough to save myself. I need You. I can't fix myself. Thank You for loving me. Thank You that Jesus died on the cross for my sins and rose from the dead. I now ask that You forgive me of all my sins. (Pause and ask them to confess silently anything specific that may be bothering them.) I surrender my life to You and ask You for eternal life. Come and live in me. I ask this in Jesus' name. Amen.

This is but one example of a *sinner's prayer*. Some people may need to pause for a while to reflect on the cross while others may celebrate the thanksgiving part of the prayer. They may express strong emotion. The prayer should not be rushed or hurried. People who express strong emotion need to have more space and less conversation. Don't be drawn into a counseling role. Simply stay with them and express unconditional love. Often the less said the better. You may just quietly say, "It's okay to be emotional. God is emotional, too."

Some may wish to pray alone. You can give them a written prayer that they can say privately when they are alone with Jesus. This gives them the opportunity to meet with God one-on-One. Later, you may want to ask them if they prayed, but be careful not to be too inquisitive. People need time to process their commitment.

Once people pray to receive Jesus, encourage them to fellowship with other believers so they can begin to grow spiritually. I try to provide a Bible in a translation they can understand. They will most likely be open to you to disciple them, so you have your work cut out for you! Try to meet with them once each week for prayer and a short Bible reading or study. Let them lead with their questions. And, if possible, invite them to your church.

Becoming a Christian is the end of the old way of life, and the beginning of an exciting new life. This is an exciting time in your life as well, because it is a great privilege to play a role in seeing people come into God's kingdom and becoming "God magnets" themselves. God deserves all of the praise!

CHAPTER 29

SOME PRACTICAL SUGGESTIONS

> But avoid foolish and ignorant disputes, knowing that they generate strife. And a servant of the LORD must not quarrel but be gentle to all, able to teach, patient, in humility correcting those who are in opposition, if God perhaps will grant them repentance, so that they may know the truth, and that they may come to their senses and escape the snare of the devil, having been taken captive by him to do his will.
>
> —2 Timothy 2:23–26

One of the most practical things you can do when sharing your faith is to avoid arguments. This does not mean you cannot *dialogue* with people. Neither does it mean that you have to agree with other people's views. It means that when they are willing to listen, you simply explain why and what you believe. A friend of mine once said that as believers we should minister in the *opposite spirit.* If others argue, we should refrain from arguing, and minister out of gentleness instead.

Scripture exhorts us to be patient, because patience is a virtue that expresses much of the character of Christ within us. We don't have to back away from confrontation, but we *do* need to approach others with humility and gentleness.

At the same time, we *are* to correct those in opposition. We are not to feel intimidated or defensive, but should quietly and confidently state our position. People will be more willing to listen if we are not combative. It is also wise to avoid passing judgment on other religions, or other people's beliefs. We don't have to agree with other religions, but we need to respect every person's right to choose his or her own beliefs.

I have told others that I accept them although I may not share their beliefs. On occasion I have even asked others to explain to me *why* they believe *what* they believe. Sometimes I will ask them what they believe about heaven and hell. Sometimes I ask what assurances they have of salvation. Then I tell them what I believe and share my faith, if they are interested.

It is always wise to remember that salvation is a process. When people receive Jesus as their Lord and Savior it is only the beginning of a wonderful journey of faith. With it will come many trials and triumphs, so make sure that new believers are encouraged to belong to a fellowship or congregation where they can grow spiritually and begin to use their gifts to minister to others.

New believers need discipleship. They need a safe place to grow. They need to learn how to read and interpret the Bible, how to pray, and how to serve God and others. We become a link to the spiritual development of others. I remember hearing Howard Hendricks say that every Christian needs a Paul, a Barnabas and a Timothy. Paul represents a spiritual father, someone who can lead us through life's challenges and mentor us into maturity. Barnabas is a colleague and friend, a peer who serves beside us as we minister the Gospel of Jesus Christ. Timothy represents a young believer, someone for us to disciple, as we become their Paul.

Bringing people into the kingdom is a joy and a lifelong commitment. God has provided many people in the church to come alongside to help in this task. When Peter was in the fishing boat and the nets were breaking, he asked for help to bring in the harvest of fish (Luke 5:6). In the same way, we come alongside to bring a harvest of souls into the kingdom of God.

These are just a few examples of the many methods I use to share the message of the Gospel, born from my own relationship and journey with Jesus Christ. You will find, as I, that as we walk with the Lord, He will open doors and give us opportunities to become ambassadors for Christ, often in unexpected, exhilarating ways. God truly wants to use each of us to bring others to Christ. God wants *you* to be a "God magnet."

Then He said to His disciples (that's us!):

> "The harvest truly *is* plentiful,
> but the laborers *are* few.
> Therefore pray the LORD of the harvest
> to send out laborers
> into His harvest."
> —Matthew 9:37–38

NOTES

1 *Merriam-Webster's Collegiate Dictionary*, 10th Edition

2 From an article endtitled "Dale Lang: A Man for Others" by Ed Hird in the July 2002, *Deep Cove Crier*, used by permission.

3 *Reader's Digest*, June 2005

4 The updated *Thompson Chain Reference Bible* has some good archeological material in it as well as the *Illustrated Encyclopedia of Bible Facts* written by J.I. Packer; Merrill C. Tenney and William White Jr., published by Nelson Bibles.

Also Available from Believe Books:

Charlene Curry

THE GENERAL'S LADY

God's Faithfulness to a Military Spouse

Charlene Curry recounts all the joys and challenges of being a career military spouse and how she triumphed over difficulties by relying on a source of spiritual power that transformed her life.

Rev. Samuel Doctorian
with Elizabeth Moll Stalcup, Ph.D.

GOD WILL NOT FAIL YOU

A Life of Miracles in the Middle East and Beyond

The miraculous life story of Rev. Samuel Doctorian, the renowned evangelist used mightily by God in the Middle East and around the world.

www.BelieveBooks.com

Major General Jerry R. Curry

FROM PRIVATE TO GENERAL

An African American Soldier Rises Through the Ranks

Major General Jerry Curry vividly describes his life journey of military missions, powerful positions, and his relationship with the true source of authority—his Father in heaven.

Fern C. Willner

WHEN FAITH IS ENOUGH

A Safari of Destiny that Reveals Principles to Live By

A faith-inspiring story of a missionary wife and mother of seven relying completely on God in the heart of Africa. *Accompanying workbook also available for discussion groups in 2007.*